HEALER'S ALMANAC
Journey into Health

GODDESS EDITION

PATRICIA SHAW

Winding Road
PUBLISHING INC.

Ferndale, Michigan

Healer's Almanac

Editor in Chief
Patty Shaw

Art Director
Nancy Smith

Copy Editors
Michelle Staver
David Shaw

Contributing Artist
Jacqueline Smith

Disclaimer

The purpose of this Almanac is to inform and entertain. The author and Winding Road Publishing shall have neither liability nor responsibility to any person with respect to any harm or loss caused or alleged by the information in this book. Many of the alternative therapies and statements are not approved by the FDA and are not intended to be given in place of sound medical advice. Please consult your physician before beginning a new treatment.

For information about submitting an article or contacting the author, address correspondences to:

Patricia Shaw
2355 Wolcott
Ferndale, MI 48220
healersalmanac@aim.com

Published by:

Winding Road Publishing, Inc.
2355 Wolcott
Ferndale, MI 48220

Cover Design by Patricia Shaw
Journal inspirations by Jacqueline Smith
Goddess Art by Patricia Shaw

ISBN 0-9741024-0-7

Printed in the United States of America.

From the Editor

Welcome to the Healer's Almanac. This book is for you, and about you, the explorer of your own potential.

Throughout our lives, we all desire to be happy and healthy. When something stops us from being in that place, we feel unwell in part of our body, mind, or soul. This Almanac offers many healing alternatives that can help bring wellness back. You will be introduced to some new therapies and reminded of some old therapies to be reconsidered. Each one of us is unique, and we have our own requirements for health and healing. All of the many options available can be combined and recombined to create a personalize recipe for creating and keeping health.

Other elements of this book are the journal pages and goddess meditations. Use them as tools to take you into your subconscious or inner world. This is where you will find your story. Much like dreams, it will be told with symbols both strange and familiar. Once you begin to understand the meaning behind the imagery found there, you will hold the key to your own healing. The journey is mysterious; be patient and use your imagination to uncover each and every clue.

Hi, my name is Patty Shaw, and I am happy to be your guide in the amazing and abundant world of alternative therapies. Join me in the exploration of these therapies, and learn more about the process of healing. It's not just for doctors anymore!

My qualifications for the job are that I am human, I have a family, and I am very curious about how we heal. Over the past seventeen years, I immersed myself in learning about the healing process. I have became a Reiki Master, an instructor of Transformational Yoga, and a Certified Spiritual Counselor through the nationally accredited Healer Development Program. In managing my own health and the health of my family, I have experienced many of the alternative therapies discussed in this almanac. I have successfully blended them with modern medicine, and we have enjoyed great results, some disappointments, but overall, no regrets. Though I won't be personally endorsing everything you read about here, I trust that you will verify these therapies for yourself. Be the authority in your life, and find the best care available for you.

You are worth it!

Table of Contents

Why 21st Century Goddesses?

What would goddesses look like if they lived today? What would be their virtues and teachings? How would they speak to us? I chose to let the values and strengths needed today define the goddesses you'll meet in this book. They'll talk to us from a place of intimacy and will validate our private feelings. Their messages will be something that will truly guide us and show us the way to achieving our personal goals.

A twenty-first century goddess is a goddess that can be seen in the actions of people all around us. Going outside the archetypical goddesses of the past, we'll look for goddesses within our own psyche, give them a voice and listen to their messages. We'll let them teach, guide and heal us through the wisdom gained from living our own lives. They'll point out all the circumstances in our lives we use to teach ourselves the things that are most important for us to learn.

Why goddesses and not gods?

Feminine energy has been re-emerging for decades and is present everywhere we look. It is waiting to be harnessed and brought to it's fullest potential within our own lives. Realizing that empowerment means acting like a goddess, we can express our feminine energy in a mature and fully actualized way.

In the past, goddesses represented the creation of life and its continuation. In humanity's early stages of development, it was all very mysterious. The goddesses' role was to explain creation and the success of life on earth. They also guided us toward socialization within our civilization. Religions and rituals were established as humanity found a way to explain its state of being. Goddesses became the foundation of security needed beneath mankind's fragile and vulnerable existence.

Gods and goddesses had come on to the scene through the imagination of men and women to create a way to shoulder the responsibility of a harsh and sometimes cruel world. They countered the extreme and unpredictable power of nature, directed the chaos and gave humans a sense of control and influence in their lives.

The goddesses found in our history are varied and versatile. They were not kept in the kitchen, nor were they barefoot and pregnant, unless they chose to be. In addition to the goddesses of life, beauty, and animals, there were goddesses of death, war, the mysteries, and the underworld. There was a goddess named to fill every role needed to support all of life. They were nurturers, teachers, healers, toilers, inventors, mothers, farmers, and merchants. Everything that we are, they were.

Looking back, I see goddesses as the guardians of a civilization that hadn't yet learned to be powerful. They were our champions of love and retribution, executing the exact actions needed that we ourselves could not do. Even the kings and queens relied on the grace of the goddesses to spare a life or bring abundance.

Behind the scenes, goddesses provided a service far beyond their specific attributes. They held our power for us. When we realize that we have power and are willing to claim it, use it responsibly as well as be responsible for it, the role of the goddess in our religions will change. It will evolve.

Goddesses not only taught us about power, they taught us about the consequences of power. The same power it takes to create, can destroy.

So, why goddesses? We need them again. We need their wisdom. We're taking steps toward our own empowerment, and they are our guides. Not because they created us, and they are helping us grow up. It's because we created them in the image of our future selves to remind us that we are not done yet. There is much more growing to do.

Just as we are different from our ancestors, today's goddesses are different, too. They have been upgrading along with us, and their usefulness is more potent if we can relate to their images. So out with Kali, the Goddess of Life and Death, and in with Kristen, the Goddess of Shadow and Light.

The virtues we will explore are not unique to women, but it is natural for us to look to women as the teachers, nurturers, and healers of our society. It is also time to bring balance and healing to a world directed and controlled predominately by male energy. Doing this through the goddess aspect will bring creative and compassionate solutions to our challenges as we transition into a life of equality.

I realize that my audience will be mostly women. A book of twenty-first century gods would not be given the attention required to take in and own the ideas within these pages. Women are turning their faces upward and deciding to heal their own souls. I just think it would be nice to find a feminine face looking back. A face that women can relate to. A face that could be their own.

I present goddesses that say. "This can be you. I'm not so far out of reach, just a few steps ahead. I'll show you the way and carry your burdens until you can."

I welcome anyone to read the messages of the goddesses. If it makes more sense to hear them from a masculine voice, rename her to Steven, Brandon, or Jake. The point is to feel supported, learn some new perspectives, and allow yourself to be helped. It's more about the message and less about the messenger. The excitement is in the journey, not just in the space of attainment.

Introduction to Alternative Therapies

There are many alternative therapies available to treat a variety of illnesses of the body, mind, and emotions. In my search for a way to heal my family and myself, I have learned that there is a great deal to choose from. I have listed and defined only a few of these therapies. My advice to you is to keep an open mind, keep searching for something that works for you, and remember no therapy is a cure all. A healthy approach to healing is balance and treating the body as a whole, not a sum of parts to be fixed or replaced individually. Prevention is the best medicine, so start early, and never stop healing yourself. I also believe that held within our bodies is the wisdom needed to bring us buoyant health. Learn to ask and then listen to your body. It will guide you and be your path to healthy living.

Acupressure

This therapy was developed in China thousands of years ago and is widely practiced in Asia today. It is a traditional Chinese medicine system which involves applying pressure with fingers or hands to strategic points along invisible meridians or pathways aligned with the body. These pathways contain a vital energy force called chi (pronounced chee), and the application of pressure to points on the body will strengthen, calm, or release blockages to the flow of energy.

There are 14 meridians, and 12 of them are bilateral, meaning that identical versions exist on both sides of the body with identical corresponding pressure points. The remaining two run along the center of the body from the top of the head to below the navel. Applying pressure carefully to chosen points can relieve symptoms, treat diseases, and improve health. Though the meridians are not part of the physical body like the nervous system or blood vessels, it has been documented through well-controlled studies that acupressure can be effective for a variety of health problems, notably nausea, pain, and weakness from stroke. Each meridian has the same name as the organ and associated bodily function that will be affected when the point is stimulated. A trained professional can administer acupressure, or it may be practiced at home. When practicing acupressure on yourself or someone else, use a steady downward pressure lasting up to two minutes. Some precautions to observe are to never apply pressure to open wounds, varicose veins, tumors, inflamed or infected skin, broken bones, or on the site of recent surgery. Avoid the abdomen, Spleen 6, and Large Intestine 4 during pregnancy.

Acupuncture

Just like acupressure, acupuncture is a traditional Chinese medicine and works with the same meridians and pressure points. The difference is a qualified professional must perform this therapy since it involves inserting hair thin needles into the pressure points. A typical treatment may involve as many as 15 needles inserted from about a fraction of an inch to about three inches into the muscle. There is little pain, though you may sense a tingling or heavy sensation as the energy blocks are released. It is well-documented that acupuncture relieves pain, and lab tests prove that endorphins are released, but scientists don't know why the pain doesn't return. Patients are just happy with the results. Acupuncture is beneficial for treating stroke damage, relieving nausea, and treating drug addiction. Acupuncture is licensed in 26 states and the District of Columbia.

Aromatherapy

The art of relaxation and healing through the use of essential oils from plants is called aromatherapy. The oil is absorbed through the skin or diffused into the air and inhaled. The essential oils are concentrated fragrant extracts from various parts of the plant. They are cold-pressed or steam-distilled, and diluted in carrier oil, such as almond or soy. They are used in massage oil, bath oil, or a diffuser, but never to be taken internally.

The fragrances act upon the brain's limbic system, which control's our memory, emotions, and hormones. A soothing and calming effect is sent throughout the body to promote self-healing.

Read more about aromatherapy in our article by Jacki Smith on pages 87-88.

Ayurvedic Medicine

This system of diagnosis and treatment was developed in India about 5,000 years ago. Ayur means life, and veda means knowledge. It is believed that stresses in our awareness or consciousness lead to unhealthy lifestyles and produce disease in our bodies. This system works with three physical properties called doshas. The first is the vata, which governs the kinetic energy of our body. It makes the heart beat, our blood flow, and activates brain and nervous system functions. The second property is kapha doshas. It is potential energy. It is responsible for physical strength and lubrication of tissues. The third property is pitta doshas. It is the governor of metabolic processes from digestion to cell functions.

The diagnostic technique is called nadi vigyan and involves taking the pulse at the wrist. This will determine if the three systems are working in harmony with each other and what is the proper treatment to bring them into balance if they are not.

Treatment involves a series of yoga postures, breathing exercises, meditation, herb supplements, specific diets, massage, and enemas. The goal is to detoxify the body and bring it back into balance.

BodyWork

The term bodywork is used to describe the family of techniques that promote relaxation and treat ailments through musculoskeletar manipulations. Many types of bodywork can be performed at home, such as Tai Chi, QiGong, Shiatsu, Massage, and Reflexology. Others like the Alexander Technique, the Feldenkras Method, Therapeutic Touch, Trager Psychophysical Integration, and Rolfing require the guidance of a trained professional.

Here are some brief descriptions of the body work techniques mentioned above.

Tai Chi: A martial art involving slow movements to improve the flow of chi throughout the body and heighten self-awareness.

Shiatsu: The Japanese version of acupressure. Finger or thumb pressure on specific body points improves the flow of chi, called ki in Japan, throughout the body.

Massage: The term massage covers an assortment of techniques which manipulate the soft tissue of the body to reduce stress and tension, increase circulation, control pain, aid in the healing of muscle and soft tissue injuries, and promote overall well being.

Reflexology: The feet and hands contain a map to the inner regions of our bodies. The gentle manipulations of specific areas on them eliminate energy blockage in the corresponding regions and bring the body to homeostasis.

The Alexander Technique: The practitioner focuses on correcting incorrect postures and habitual body movements that are believed to damage or impair the body's function.

The Feldenkrais Method: New patterns of movement are taught through voice command, touch, and exercises to improve posture, movement, and breathing.

Rolfing: Also known as Structural Integration, retrains the body to perform everyday activities with less stress by using deep massage of the connective tissues and movement exercises. It is beneficial for emotional and physical health.

Therapeutic Touch: Despite the name, there is no physical touching in this therapy. The practitioner moves their hands in a slow sweeping movement about six inches over your body detecting energy blockages in the aura (the energy field that surrounds the body) and works to remove them. A twenty minute session will leave you feeling relaxed and give you relief from pain.

Trager Psychophysical Integration: Designed to detect and correct chronic stress patterns in the body that effect posture and movement. Gentle rocking, touch, shaking, and directed exercises have proven to help patients with neuromuscular problems caused by injury or illness like muscular sclerosis or muscular dystrophy.

Chiropractic

Licensed and practiced in all 50 states, Chiropractic medicine has earned its acceptance because of its proven effectiveness in treating back pain and all its related complications.

Chiropractic theory states that the nervous system plays a significant role in maintaining health and that subluxations or problems in the joints interfere with its proper functioning and resulting health problems occur. Through manual manipulations of the spine, joints, and muscles, chiropractors seek to bring the body back into balance. Read our article written by a licensed chiropractor on page 24 for more information.

Many private insurance plans, Medicaid, and Medicare cover chiropractic visits in most states.

Cranial Sacral

Cranio Sacral Therapy (CST) was developed 30 years ago by Dr. John Upledger of Michigan State University. This technique is practiced by osteopaths, dentists, physical therapists, occupational therapists, acupuncturists, and licensed body workers to relieve headaches and help heal damaged tissue and chronic infections. Surrounding the brain and spinal column is a fluid called cerebrospinal fluid. It cycles from the top of the head or cranium to the tip of the tailbone or sacrum and back again. In a healthy body, it moves and flows with the assistance of membranes without resistance. A disease or injury can damage the membrane and limit flow of cerebrospinal fluid to the nerve trunks along the spine. This form of malnutrition to the core nervous system and brain can result in many different diseases and malfunctions in the body. A cranial sacral therapist can detect where the fluid is inhibited and by light touch can release the block, assisting the body to return to its natural rhythms. The benefits of cranial sacral work are improved brain and spinal cord functions, enhanced vitality, and resistance to disease. A typical session lasts about one hour, and results can be felt within a few hours.

Homeopathy

Based on the assumption that like cures like, German physician Samuel Hahnemann developed the concept that substances that cause illness in a healthy person will cure the same symptoms in a person who is sick. He then developed a method of "potentizing" the remedies. By diluting the remedy in a water alcohol solution and vigorously shaking it, Hahnemann believed the side effects would greatly be minimized, and the benefit will then be greatly maximized. Over the past 200 years, over 2,000 remedies have been developed for our use. Homeopathic remedies are available over-the-counter at health food stores and other specialty stores. For "constitutional" healing or the healing of chronic problems in your core makeup, it is recommended you seek the assistance of a licensed Homeopathic Practitioner. Homeopathic Practitioners usually have prior medical training in addition to their homeopathic training.

Learn more about adding homeopathic remedies to your first aid kit in our article by Laura Lohman-Gannan, RSHom(NA), CCH on page 109.

Mind Body Therapies

These therapies focus on the connection between the mind and the body with the goal to promote overall healing through mental and physical activities.

Biofeedback: You are trained to change and control body functions such as heart rate, skin temperature, muscle tension, and brain activity with the use of computerized machines.

Guided Imagery: The practice of imagining scenarios that may influence physical conditions within the body. Patients have reported physical and psychological benefits.

Hypnotherapy: Conducted by a trained professional, a client is placed in a deep state of relaxed, focused awareness. Positive suggestions are then made by the hypnotherapist to help the client improve mental and physical conditions.

Meditation: A technique used to create deep relaxation in the body and mind by doing mental exercises with closed eyes and focused concentration. An altered state of awareness can be achieved, and like hypnosis, you can make changes in your own body and mind for improved health and enlightenment.

Support Groups: A group of people with similar illnesses or traumatic experiences come together to share ideas and feelings. The group is commonly led by a trained psychotherapist. The psychological benefits include increased self-esteem, compassion, and acceptance.

Yoga: Body postures, breathing, and stretching are performed in a sequence to calm the mind, relax the body, and release toxins from the soft tissues. Yoga will also give you more flexibility and strength.

Spirituality: The practice of contemplating spiritual values outside a religious context. It brings a source of relaxation, contentment, self-awareness, and often healing to the mind and soul.

Naturopathic Medicine

This therapy is based on three principles.

1. Help the body heal itself.
2. Find the root cause of illness instead of treating symptoms.
3. Avoid therapies that cause damage to the body, such as toxic drugs and surgery.

Naturopathic doctors use homeopathy, herbal remedies, traditional Chinese medicine, chiropractic adjustments, nutrition, massage, and exercise to bring the body into balance so it can heal itself. They also take into consideration their patient's lifestyle because they believe attitudes and spirituality, in addition to the physical components, play an integral part in the onset of disease. Currently, Naturopathic doctors are licensed to practice in nine states. Many other states allow them to practice in a limited way. They study at four year accredited medical schools. The first two years are spent studying the same core science studies as regular medical schools. The second two years are focused on training in Naturopathic healing techniques.

Resources

Looking for an alternative health practitioner is a process of exploration. You will find them through referrals, in the phone book, through advertisements in health and spiritual publications, and on the internet. Use the title of the modality you are interested in as your keyword. We have a resource section at the end of this book to help you get started.

How to Use This Calendar and Journal

Making the Most of the Calendar and Journal

This Almanac is not just for you, it is about you. As you read through the information, participate in the meditations, and follow the rituals, record your feelings and experiences on the blank journal pages. Include as much detail as you can, even if it seems insignificant or "you just made it up". Upon later reflection, those seemingly unimportant ideas may be the keys you're looking for to unlock the mysteries of your subconscious mind. Another way to use the journal pages is to contemplate the provided inspirations and write about what they mean to you.

As you follow the chapters, they weave through the year, inviting you to take part in the cycle of life. Let them bring you closer to knowing the intimate connections you have to the Earth, our solar system, and ultimately, yourself. This book will reveal your story one chapter at a time and take you on a journey into health.

Each chapter focuses on one month of the calendar year. There is information on the changing seasons and several different ways to enhance or diminish the impact they have on our lives.

I have also included "Living With Moon Energy" as a way to track the influences the New and Full Moon has on us as she travels through the zodiac constellations. Record your activities and moods in the space provided. You'll be surprised to find what the Moon can nudge you into. Be prepared, and beat her at her own game the next time she lumbers through a familiar zodiac sign.

Finally, we have goddess meditations for you to participate in and some opportunities to make twelve new powerful friends. We all need guidance, advice, or some plain old healing from time to time, and much can be learned from the messages of these model women. Consult the goddesses on your most private and pertinent matters, and they will have the most enlightening counsel for you. Use the journal pages to record your experiences and personal messages. Periodically return to reread the wisdom. It will unfold for you in a new way each time.

Even though we began this almanac in January, you may start the book in any month and follow the chapters until you make your way through an entire year. The circle of life has no beginning and no end, so jump in anywhere.

Enjoy the journal and fill the pages with you!

Winter

December 21st–March 20th
Season of Sleep and Purification

Whether you live in a climate that chases you indoors for warmth or one that doesn't really change at all, the energy of the winter season is one of rest, review, and renewal. This is the part of the cycle of life that gives us the time and space needed to look at our lives, plan for changes, and rebuild ourselves from the inside out. Rest is the key component, and nature gifts us with shorter days and longer nights to help us achieve this.

Native American spirituality looks to the White Buffalo for inspiration and guidance during the winter months. It represents evolution and perfection. Let this magnificent animal purify you, body, mind, and spirit by inviting it into your meditations. Also, use sweetgrass smudge in your rituals to carry your intentions to heaven.

Suggestions for Optimal Seasonal Health

Physical To combat viral infections, take extra vitamin C, garlic, and CoQ 10. Check out our homeopathic flu and cold remedies article, get plenty of rest and fresh air, drink fluids, keep the house clean, disinfect and wash hands often. Eat foods seasonal for your climate. It will help your body stay warm and conserve energy.

Emotional SAD (seasonal affective disorder) happens when there's not enough sunlight or daylight hours to keep you happy. To help alleviate the symptoms, purchase some full spectrum light bulbs, take vitamins D and B-complex to combat depression, get outdoors on sunny days at noon, exercise often, and paint rooms a light color. Do what you can to get as much natural light into the house as possible, or take a vacation to the tropics.

Mental To reduce stress from spending too much money on gifts, try the credit card interest rate juggle and plan a budget you can live with.

Spiritual Explore the spiritual world within for answers which give peace of mind and some quiet time alone. Try this abbreviated meditation technique. Find a quiet place where you won't be disturbed for at least 30 minutes. Breath deeply and slowly until you feel yourself drifting gently and the chatter in your mind stops. Bring your focus to your center; visualize it as a bright sun. Here resides your divinity. Ask for guidance or just sit and receive unconditional love. When you are done, ask your chakras to balance for the next thing you will be doing. Slowly become fully aware of the room. Wiggle your toes and yawn.

What Once was Old is Made New Again

By Patty Shaw

I was nearly 5 when I learned the meaning of the "New Year". By the time I lived my first decade, I understood the genius of making resolutions. I would look back at the past year, pick out a few things I'd like to do differently, and promise to be faithful. In my mind, the New Year brought exciting possibilities, and all in the past was forgiven, well at least forgotten. Yes, in my youth and innocence, just changing my mind about myself made me feel new again.

Now that I'm in my 5th decade, I have much more baggage, and it all seems so complicated. The thought of starting a new year seemed like an invitation to add to the pile rather than a fresh start. It occurred to me that I had to make a few changes to my New Year resolution process.

Experience taught me that events forgotten don't magically disappear never to be heard from again. They collected in my body as memories and solidified into distant echoes that came back around to make themselves known when the correct triggers were tripped. Much like booby traps, they would go off. Old reactions and patterns were alive and well, running all over my neatly planned and executed resolutions.

I learned that situations were freeze-framed in my body, replaying their stories over and over again. How can the old become new again when a random act of life sets off past behavior patterns that I resolved to change? Worse yet, I felt powerless over them. I had to learn how to make changes in every level of me in order for my desired changes to be real and lasting.

Unlike when I was a child, changing was not just a mental or willful process. It involved my body, my emotions, and my soul as well. Old, unresolved hurts needed to be remembered, given compassion and forgiveness, and allowed to "grow up" and be made aware that I am no longer in that time and space.

To heal these patterns in myself, I had to set them free by giving them a voice, then show them that I'm no longer a victim or powerless. Finally, I needed to forgive myself and anyone else involved. As I let go of the past with love and forgiveness, I created a clean foundation for my new resolutions.

I have found that the parts of my past that haunted me just wanted me to remember them so they could be healed. This way I could go forward in my life unencumbered by sadness and pain. I consider them my friends and their gift to me, is Me! When I am successful at this, I can truly feel what was old is new again. My innocence is renewed!

Try affirming, with an open heart, that you are loved and forgiven (of everything). Feel yourself lighten up as tension flows out of your body with a few tears. Then pick one other person and tell them that they are loved and forgiven. Watch as the burden of guilt lifts out of their eyes. What a wonderful way to start the year.

On the following pages you will be introduced to Rebecca, the Goddess of Responsibility. She embodies beauty, love, and honesty. She is here to help you see your own strength and develop personal responsibility. To prepare for making this connection with Rebecca, spend some time in this meditation. It will help you create a place in your life for what you desire.

In a quiet place where you will be undisturbed for about an hour, sit comfortably and begin to relax. With eyes closed, inhale through your nose deeply for the count of four. Then hold your breath for four counts and then exhale through your mouth for four counts. Then pause for four more counts before inhaling again. Do this three or four times before returning to regular breathing.

With each cycle of deep breathing, feel your body becoming more and more relaxed. Mentally suggest to each muscle group in your body that they relax with each breath and that they release tension with each exhale.

Once you feel relaxed, imagine that a beautiful white light surrounds you. Allow it to calm you and give you a feeling of security. Acknowledge that you are in complete control, and though you can stop this meditation at any time, you wish to go into a deeper relaxed state to access clearer self-awareness.

Next, ask that you be sent a loving guardian angel or spirit guide that wants to be with you and heal you while you explore a repeating pattern in your life that is no longer working for you.

Bring to mind this old, outdated life pattern and ask that you be made aware of what personal beliefs caused you to attract this situation over and over again, to react in the same way, getting the same undesirable results. If you don't get an answer or understanding right away, try rephrasing the question or invite an answer to come to you later in a very obvious and gentle way.

Once you are satisfied with your visualization and are ready to move on, state that this behavior, attitude, or belief no longer works for you and is blocking you in your goal for a successful and happy life. Affirm that you learned from this experience and are ready to live your life free of these old unhealthy patterns. Note: be specific and be positive. For example, . . . I am ready to live my life free because I am loveable, or I am smart, or I am healthy, or I believe in myself, or I am trustworthy, and others have confidence in me.

Many times we need support when changing a belief about ourselves, especially when we are reclaiming our power. For help, call Archangel Michael to come and dissolve the old beliefs or write a new "contract" for you to live by until you are confident you have empowered yourself in this way completely. Use the same positive affirmations you stated earlier. If you feel it is necessary, ask for a spirit helper to be sent to work with you while you build this positive

continued on page 146

January

What once was old is made new again.

Some Things To Do This Month

Clear your body of toxins by drinking fresh-squeezed vegetable juice. Do aerobic exercises to sweat out the toxins.

Use meditation to develop your psychic abilities or look inward for your answers to problems.

Get your house in order by healing family strife with honesty and fairness. This is not the time for stubborn pride.

Living With Moon Energy

The Moon is the closest heavenly body to our planet. Her affect on us is real and immediate. Tracking the phases of the Moon and the zodiac sign she is traveling through can map out a cause and effect cycle for us. It will help make sense of our mood swings and patterns of luck, both good and bad.

Look up the Moon table on page 151 and record the date and zodiac sign the New and Full Moons are in.

Next, write down how you felt the three days around the New and Full Moons. Also record what was happening in your life at these times. Keeping track of this information will help you anticipate and prepare for future influences from the Moon. You may also compare your life with the interpretations provided on page 148.

Notes on how the energy of the New Moon and Full Moon affect me.

January's Goddess

The New Age is about being responsible for ourselves. This means the ability to respond to our needs, fears, health, and every other event in our lives that affects our destiny. We are learning to take care of our business, make choices, and own the outcome. This is truly an empowered way of thinking and acting.

When we respond to pain by looking for someone to blame, we are limiting our choices, growth, and creativity. We then miss the opportunity to learn from the experience and improve the consistency of our soul.

To learn more about yourself and how being responsible will help you improve your quality of life, connect with Rebecca in this meditation.

Meditation: Prepare your meditation space by turning off phones and pagers, setting a glass of water near you, and dimming the lights. Next, light a candle, and light your favorite incense or spritz some perfume. Sit in a comfortable chair with your feet on the floor, legs uncrossed.

Begin by breathing deeply, slowly, and rhythmically. Try a four-count rhythm. Inhale slowly for a count of four, hold your breath for a count of four, and then exhale for a count of four. Repeat this until you feel relaxed and your mind is quiet.

Once you feel relaxed, let your breathing return to normal, and let your attention go to your midsection. Visualize the flame of a candle illuminating the center of your body. As you focus on it, connect with it. Feel its warmth and brightness filling you with inner strength. Ask the light to merge with you and fill your entire body. Then, let it continue to expand and fill the space around your body to about three feet around you.

This is your sacred space. Within it, you do your creating. Now, ask your light to reach out to Rebecca, the Goddess of Responsibility and connect with her for support and inspiration. Once you feel connected, ask a question or just spend time receiving her gifts. When you are ready to move on, end the meditation by disconnecting from the goddess with gratitude and say goodbye. Return to the present by becoming focused on your body and the room. Wiggle your toes and take a drink of water. Imagine your sacred space coming in close to your body and the brilliant light minimizing to the size of a candle flame in your midsection.

Next, jot down the ideas, feelings, or images you received on the following journal pages. As you analyze the information, keep in mind your question. If you didn't have a question, try to relate your information to what is going on in your life today.

Rebecca *Goddess of Responsibility*

In January 2000, a New Age began. You closed the door on victimization, powerlessness, and blame forever and began to look to yourself for salvation. It's a great evolutionary step for humanity, and you'll have many growing pains. I am here to help. I am the goddess of the New Age, and my essence is Responsibility. I am perpetually innocent, and I bring the gift of rejuvenation to burned out lives. I am courageous, and I face fear, hatred, and darkness with unconditional love and forgiveness. I am clever and inspire with beauty, tenderness, humor, and honesty. I heal with my ability to teach you to look within and build the foundation of your life on truth, and not the shifting sands of illusion. Change requires patience, compassion, and courage. Lean on me and ask for assistance as you transform yourself and ease into the adventure of personal freedom that being responsible for yourself brings.

I understand the complexities of a changing life. I will help you stand strong while you refocus and become the responsible being you are.

J A N U A R Y

Within the creation of the Universe,
I am reunited with my true path and destiny

What once was old is made new again

Even though you may never know
how far it is to the heart of your truth,
journey on.

Give me moments to see and places to feel.

What once was old is made new again

One day of smiles and laughter, one day out of a thousand days can change your life forever.

What is Quantum Techniques?

By Stephen Daniel

Quantum techniques brings together four incredibly powerful, natural healing modalities. The first is the scanning of voice patterns. We are able, through the development of new advancements in voice scanning, to evaluate a person's energy field over the phone. This allows for easy and rapid access to treatment. Voice testing may be the easiest and most accessible form of bioenergetic diagnostic testing. Dr. Savely Yurkovsky, M.D.,

> **"The quantum protocol changes the destructive frequencies in the body to healthy frequencies causing healing."**

founder of Field Control Therapy in New York City, says that "bioenergetics diagnostic testing, if done right, is the most accurate diagnostic testing in existence." The second dynamic tool is using bioenergetics scanning of voice patterns to determine all possible components of a problem, physical and non-physical. The third tool we use is a healing code consisting of meridian and chakra points. From the voice scanning, we are able to diagnose the energetic disturbances in the person's field and give them a unique acupressure code for their system and their present issue. They then tap out the simple code on their body. This com-

pletely balances their energy field and changes the destructive frequencies within the body. The fourth tool we use in Quantum Techniques is called the quantum protocol. The quantum protocol is a series of input/out switches on the body that change the destructive frequencies in the body to healthy frequencies causing healing. The protocol puts the body into a profoundly deep healing and meditative state. In that state, the body immediately begins to detoxify and heal itself.

The combination of these four powerful tools can help free you from the bonds of physical and emotional problems - quickly, easily, and forever. Quantum techniques utilizes the best of these techniques and brings you a complete treatment: removal of problems, elimination of toxins, blocks to the body's energy system, and energetic clearing of the body's detoxifying systems.

How do you find the components and what are they?

By using our new process of voice scanning, we scan through more than 6,000 possible components of any problem, physical or non-physical, within 5 minutes. This includes all environmental toxins, biological toxins, pharmacological toxins, deregulations of the body's energy system in the body, all major organs, all body systems (literally everything that's in the body), hundreds of emotions, spiritual issues, mental issues, relational issues, belief issues, etc. Literally almost anything that could be part of your problem.

Normally, over the course of treatment, we will identify 50-100 components of your problem, no matter if it is physical or non-physical. The identification of these components is absolutely essential to healing. There is nowhere else on the planet that we are aware of where you can identify the components of your problem, completely within 5 minutes and over the phone. Once all the components and their destructive frequencies have been determined, you will be give both an acupressure code and quantum protocol to change these destructive frequencies to healthy frequencies.

How does healing take place?

We believe the creator has placed a healing code into every cell of our bodies. The scanning of the biofield through the voice allows us to find that unique code and then input into the body that code, sometimes by tapping and sometimes just by reading. The code clears all disturbances in the energy field and clears destructive frequencies. The code is a combination of meridian and chakra points. The Quantum protocol is a system of seven major fuse boxes in the body, that to our knowledge, have never been discovered before. Several of these fuse boxes contain multiple switches or circuit breakers. In fact, one of the fuse boxes contains 120 switches or circuits.

By flipping the correct switches in the correct order, it uses the body's energy system to fix the problem. It appears these switches allow direct access to the unconscious for reprogramming destructive images and beliefs. The protocol puts the body into a deep healing mode, and healing occurs as unhealthy frequencies are changed to healthy ones. The odds of accidentally discovering the correct protocol and codes are less than one in a billion. That is why it is so critical to scan the voice for the exact codes and protocol.

How effective is QT?

In our experience, Quantum Techniques is by far the most effective form of treatment for most non-physical problems. For physical issues, Quantum Techniques is the most effective form of alternative therapy that we are aware of, and many times will be effective when all traditional means have been exhausted and the problem still exists. Many people experience dramatic or complete relief, especially of emotional issues immediately or within minutes. Many physical issues, because of the physical mass involved, take longer.

Is there any research that Quantum Techniques really works?

First of all is our clients reports. We will treat anyone and let them think about it overnight. If they don't feel they were dramatically helped, they call us the next day, and there is no charge. We have over a 95% success rate.

Secondly is the results from Heart Rate Variability Studies (HRV). Heart Rate

Variability (HRV) is the most stable diagnostic measure of the body's autonomic nervous system. It has been a staple of traditional medicine for more than 30 years and is not even 1% susceptible to the placebo effect.

Recent pre and post studies have indicated consistently that a Quantum Techniques session has a dramatic positive effect on the autonomic nervous system and on body chemistry. In fact, Peter Julian, the director of Advanced Cardiologics in Colorado, recently commented that these treatments "consistently do what the medical profession and research on HRV say is impossible. It almost always, instantly balances the autonomic nervous system."

The autonomic nervous system is responsible for controlling 80% of all body functions (everything that happens automatically) and is very resistant to any rapid change. Chronic imbalance in the body's autonomic nervous system has been found to lead to disease states as well as mental and emotional disorders.

We are collecting data from Dark Field Microscopy. Dark Field Microscopy is a newer mainstream medical diagnostic procedure that is a special type of blood test. It can show the state of a person's blood as well as the presence of virus, bacteria, the state of the proteins, vitamin and mineral deficiencies, enzyme deficiencies, etc. Dark Field is also not even 1% susceptible to the placebo effect. Initial data indicate pre and post treatment slides with a Quantum Techniques session show dramatic and immediate changes in the blood. That is why we can routinely balance a person's field who is fighting a virus

or bacteria and have them symptom free in a few short hours

How do I get started with Quantum Techniques?

Initially we fax, email, or mail a copy of our treatment manual to a person to study. After a few short minutes, they can learn the system. We have worked with 10 year old children unassisted who have easily mastered the system. Our first session is typically around 10 minutes as we stay on the phone while the person taps out the healing codes. Subsequent treatments typically take 2 to 4 minutes per issue to give a healing code. The client gets off the phone and then taps out the code and does the protocol. Most clients notice an immediate result in all but the most chronic and difficult physical issues. The following list is a small example of the many things that respond to this exciting new work: ADD, ADHD, addiction, allergies, anger, anxiety, asthma, bacterial infection, child abuse victims, chronic fatigue, chronic pain, dental fears, depression, eating disorders, environmental illness, fibromyalgia, flying fears, grief, guilt, headaches, hormone imbalances, migraines, OCD, public speaking, rape/trauma, rejection, sexual problems, stress, stuttering, surgical and medical fears, tinnitus, viruses, war/other trauma.

Currently there are only three practitioners worldwide doing this exciting new work. We are currently training two other practitioners and have developed the first in a videotape series to train others. You can reach Dr. Daniel or Dr. Moses at 888-767-8002. More information is available at: www.quantumtechniques.com.

Still Cleaning Up The Mess From Last Year

What did we start in January by allowing ourselves to be forgiven of everything? Is it possible or even legal? Believe me, I am familiar with the roller coaster of reactions you may be riding. My big question was always, what do we do with all the anger, guilt, and resentment? We surrender them to the transformational power of love. All you need is love. John Lennon was right! So, clean up those emotions that range from guilt to revenge one at a time with unconditional love.

Let's do a meditation together to experience the power of unconditional love. Whenever I'm feeling lost or depressed, I do this meditation. It's very effective in helping me destress and keep from overreacting. You can make a tape of this meditation and play it whenever you need it. Speak slowly and pause between each step to give your imagination time to build the visualization.

In a quiet private place, make yourself comfortable. You will need about one hour to complete this meditation. Wear soft, loose clothing and bring in a few elements that will add to your relaxation without being distracting. For example, play soft mood music in the background or keep lightly scented oil or incense nearby and turn the lights low.

Close your eyes and inhale deeply through your nose for the count of four. Hold your breath for the count of four and then release your breath through your mouth as if you are gently blowing out birthday candles for the count of four. While repeating this breathing pattern, suggest to your body that all your muscles relax more and more with each breath. After three cycles of elongated breathing, begin to imagine breathing in feelings of love and acceptance. With each exhale, imagine letting go of stress and tension and worries of the day. Do this for three more cycles and really feel your body becoming heavier and more relaxed. Affirm that this feels wonderful and that you are in a safe and peaceful place. You are now ready to begin your meditation.

Imagine you are a tree. Your strong roots grow out from your tailbone and feet, traveling deep into the earth. Let your roots go wide also. They will act as stabilizers when the wind begins to blow.

Imagine your roots have gone so deep into the earth that they have tapped into a river. It is the river of eternal life that flows through the center of the earth. It sparkles with life and feels very nurturing. You react instantly and begin to draw up the sparkling water into your roots. Watch as the sparkling water rises up your roots and into your feet.

As you drink it up, it fills your body. This water is very light and feels more like air than water. It's very relaxing, yet strengthening at the same time, and you welcome it. Soon you feel your body becoming saturated by the sparkling water, and it begins to overflow into the space around you. Notice it doesn't go any farther than three feet around your body. A complete space is created around you in the shape of an egg. It sparkles and glows, and makes you feel safe.

You now begin to grow branches out from your arms and head. Brilliant white flowers begin to bloom all along the branches. The flowers begin to attract a gentle luminescence from above you. It flows into the blooms and then into your body, filling you to overflowing.

The luminescence then fills the space around you the same way the sparkling water did. All you can see is the glow around you and in you.

After you bask in the light for awhile, your attention is drawn to your midsection as a soft light starts to glow in the area of your stomach. It's yellow and feels warm.

You become aware that it is a part of you, and you feel comforted by this. Your light continues to grow and fill your entire body to overflowing, and when it does, it bursts out into the space around you, mingling and merging with the light from the Earth and Heaven.

You feel that this space is all your own. No one or nothing can come in unless you invite them. As you declare this in your mind, you notice a blue edge form at the perimeter of your space. You are completely surrounded by it. You feel protected.

Your attention is drawn back to your body. Now you notice some patches of darkness. They feel out of place somehow. You wish to bring light to them, you know it will make you content, and you desire it.

Be gentle with yourself. You don't have to scrub yourself like you're a stained kitchen sink. Invite the healing of unconditional love into your body. It will transform those dark places like the effortless action of bleach fading away those seemingly stubborn stains.

Just allow it to flow through you and surrender your hurts over to a higher love. After these darker areas are filled with light and are stable, rinse well with a good cry to release related emotions, and blow it all dry with a cleansing hearty laugh. Ask the light within you to balance you for the next thing you are going to do.

Once you feel complete with this, you may release the light or ask it to stay with you the rest of the day. Come fully present in the room by stretching and slowly opening your eyes. Wiggle your toes, yawn, and drink a sip of water. Welcome back.

I was born under the sign of Cancer the Crab. This is important for you to know because there is a little crab in all of us. I resisted being typecast and denied having any personality traits common with the Crab, but alas, I act like a crab more often than I'd like to admit. I've caught myself side-stepping issues like a crab running from a predator along the beach. I have found myself hanging on to

continued on page 146

February

Still cleaning up the mess from last year.

Some Things To Do This Month

Develop your ability to adjust to any situation; it will help reduce stress.

Continue to get enough rest and cleanse yourself spiritually, emotionally, and mentally, with journaling, meditation, and talking with a good friend or a professional.

Support clearing your body of toxins by eating a healthy diet and staying away from processed foods.

Living With Moon Energy

The Moon is the closest heavenly body to our planet. Her affect on us is real and immediate. Tracking the phases of the Moon and the zodiac sign she is traveling through can map out a cause and effect cycle for us. It will help make sense of our mood swings and patterns of luck, both good and bad.

Look up the Moon table on page 151 and record the date and zodiac sign the New and Full Moons are in.

Next, write down how you felt the three days around the New and Full Moons. Also record what was happening in your life at these times. Keeping track of this information will help you anticipate and prepare for future influences from the Moon. You may also compare your life with the interpretations provided on page 148.

Notes on how the energy of the New Moon and Full Moon affect me.

February's Goddess

Living in balance is something we are all advised to do. It keeps us healthier, happier, and we feel we have more energy throughout the day. With all the demands on us, at times, balance is a fantasy. We live in a world of chaos, including jobs, family, and vacations. All of it takes planning and concentrated effort to accomplish. So, how do we achieve balance? We begin by valuing it. See it as something as necessary as the air we breathe. Those of us who have forgotten how to be in balance can call upon Meredith for her teachings. Do the following meditation to begin a private tutorial on balance and how you can achieve it in your life.

Meditation: For this meditation, you will need two candles, one white or light candle, one black or dark candle (they will represent the two extremes of balance), a glass of water for drinking later, a straight backed chair, a fresh rosebud in a vase of water, and a favorite incense or perfume.

When you are ready to begin, dim the lights, light the candles and incense, close your eyes, and begin the slow rhythmic breathing. Once you feel relaxed and your mind is quiet, return your breathing to a natural pace and focus on the brilliant glow in the center of your body. Imagine it expanding and filling your entire body and aura. Imagine a blue edge of light forming at the perimeter of your aura and affirm that you are inside your sacred space. You are loved and protected, and in total control of events happening here.

Once you are satisfied with your set-up, you may proceed to creating a connection with Meredith, the Goddess of Balance. Imagine your inner light extending a light bridge into the heart of the universe. On this bridge stands a man or a woman on your behalf with an invitation to Meredith to come and talk with you. Soon you will feel a presence. Ask if it is Meredith. You will recognize her energy as uplifting, non-judgmental, and gentle. If it is not, ask your guide on the bridge to send this energy away and call to Meredith again. When you feel ready, begin asking your questions. You may ask for advice about a situation or just allow her to bring balance into your life. Let her energy teach you and heal you. Spend as much time as you need with Meredith.

When you feel complete with your conversation with Meredith, ask her to place her essence in the rosebud, and as it blooms, you will understand her advice fully. Thank her for her gifts and release her. Return to your waking life by focusing on your body and begin stretching and moving. Open your eyes, sip some water, and reflect on your meditation. You may want to write down your experience in the journal pages before you begin to forget. Remember to record the feelings, pictures, and smells, too. This will help you recognize Meredith the next time you meet.

Meredith
Goddess of Balance

I have watched you struggle with choice. I feel the intense emotions that influence your decisions. I see you pit logic against desire. I understand the need to bring balance into your life, and I hold the key. Let me teach you the beauty of discernment and how it will set you on a course of focus, protection, and fulfillment.

I am the force that steadies the pendulum that swings from one extreme to another. I am the black that merges with the white that becomes the grey areas where a life lived in balance exists.

When your life becomes too chaotic, and you feel out of control, call to me, and I will breathe my gentle breath of compassion. It will quiet your confusion and calm your nerves.

I will listen to your heart and help bring those desires to your consciousness.

Once you understand what is in your heart, you will know what it is you need to do to create balance in your life.

The world you live in is a continual dance of light and dark. Let me bring a balanced mind and heart to all your decisions.

Lift my spirits and help me be strong, so that I learn your healing song.

Still cleaning up after last year

*It is time for change in my life. Will I make a clean break
or will I slide back into the past like a familiar pair
of old bluejeans?*

F E B R U A R Y

Allow your good intentions to disperse and transform any stress or tension into expanding love.

Still cleaning up after last year

Finding peace in a hectic life involves taking time to illuminate your spirit.

What Does Chiropractic Medicine Have to Offer?

by Stacy L. Winn, D.C.

Every man, woman, and child's health status today is the direct result of their habits, thoughts, feelings and actions. Virtually all of the circumstances of their life affect their physical condition. That is a very profound statement, and since you are reading this almanac, chances are very good that you are ready to make some changes in at least one area of your life. Chiropractic can help.

"Imagine that your brain is the main command center. From the main command center runs a cable, your spinal cord, down the command chain."

Have you ever wondered if a Chiropractor is really a Doctor? The education required to become a Doctor of Chiropractic is extensive. A degree in Chiropractic medicine requires a minimum of six years of academic study in addition to an internship. The number of hours of classroom instruction for both Chiropractic colleges and Medical colleges is about the same. A Doctor of Chiropractic is required to pass national board examinations before we can be licensed to practice, just like our medical counterparts. The major difference is that Doctors of

Chiropractic believe that the power that made the body can heal the body and address health and healing in a more holistic way. We consider the whole person and their lifestyle in addition to their symptoms when diagnosing a treatment.

The diagnostic exam is different than a typical physical, but it tells us a lot about you, your body, and how well you are coping with your current lifestyle. Chiropractic examinations allow us to find spinal misalignments known as vertebral subluxations. Subluxations irritate your nervous system and are the cause of pain or the symptoms you may be experiencing.

Imagine that your brain is the main command center. From the main command center runs a cable, your spinal cord, down the command chain. This cable is protected by a series of stacked interlocking pieces, called vertebrae. Between each segment, there is a shock absorber called a disk. The combination of vertebrae and disks allow for movement of the command cable without damage or trauma to the cable.

Attached to the vertebrae are the ribs, and exiting from between the vertebrae are 31 main nerve bundles that send messages from the main command center through the nerve bundles further down the command chain. Similar to telephone wires, reaching each and every area of the body, your nerve bundles control everything from the involuntary blink to the decision and ability to smile.

Now, if one or more of these main 31 phone lines (nerve bundles) gets interrupted due to one or more of the interlocking pieces (vertebra) being out of alignment (vertebral subluxation), not all the main command messages get through to the appropriate parts of the body, thus causing nerve interference. At this point, the body will try to reroute messages to keep things running smoothly. However, the system is stressed, and it will produce sensations we call symptoms.

Symptoms are the body's warning system, a way of communicating that there is a problem, much like the indicator lights in our cars. Typically when the lights go on, you've already got a serious problem. The two most common symptoms that cause people to seek out a Doctor of Chiropractic are low back pain and many types of headaches. People are surprised to learn about the other symptoms that typically resolve themselves once their spine is back in alignment.

For over 100 years, Doctors of Chiropractic have successfully treated patients suffering from asthma, migraines, sinusitis, bed wetting, chronic ear infections, hyperactivity, ADD, ADHD, learning disabilities, fibromyalgia, numbness in hands, growing pains in children, TMJ, reflux, colic, whiplash, even birth- for both mother and babe, as well as many other symptoms and disorders

or traumas. Chiropractors remove nerve interference and allow the body to do the rest. It is amazing what the body can do without nerve interference. Through spinal adjustments, Doctors of Chiropractic eliminate the nerve interferences that cause the problems and symptoms. Without interference, the body is able to recuperate and function at its maximum capacity.

"Chiropractic patients find that they are better able to withstand the onslaught of stresses thrown at them in their daily lives."

Spinal adjustments also allow the body's immune system to operate at its very best. The body will then heal itself naturally. Chiropractors focus on proper skeletal alignment as an option to using over-the-counter or prescribed medications to treat pain. The exclusive use of drugs could suppress the symptoms and cheat the body out of an opportunity to correct the problem on its own.

The best use of Chiropractic medicine is to use it as a preventative health care system. Our goal as Doctors of Chiropractic is to keep the body subluxation free, therefore working at its maximum potential. Chiropractic patients find that they are better able to withstand the onslaught of stresses thrown at them in their daily lives. Stresses that can cause subluxations fall into three major categories: physical, emotional, and chemical. Physical stresses are traumas to the body caused by auto accidents, slips, falls, violence, or sport injury. The emotional component is due to a life style change trauma like divorce, loss of a job, or death. Have you ever noticed that your family and friends tend to be sick after a death in the family, caring for an injured loved one, or a divorce? The final component is chemical, and this is the most difficult to manage. The air we breath and the water we consume are often the biggest challenges we face in this regard, followed closely by the American diet.

"Today, as many as six million Americans have limited mobility due to back, hip, and leg pain, at a yearly cost of over 40 billion dollars."

At this point, you may be wondering how Doctors of Chiropractic remove this nerve interference. There are several different techniques out there, almost as many as there are Chiropractors. Most techniques involve your Chiropractor diagnosing which bones in your spine are out of alignment and in which direction they are misaligned. Gently using their hands or an instrument, the bones are adjusted and brought back into their proper alignment.

Your Doctor of Chiropractic will discuss a care plan with you that is your personal path to recovering optimal health. It can take just a few adjustments or many adjustments depending on the severity of your condition to get past the symptoms and to the root problem causing the symptoms. You did not get sick overnight, nor will health return spontaneously. Your symptoms

(warning lights) are the last to come and the first to leave, so follow your care plan faithfully to avoid relapses into your previous symptoms.

I place a lot of emphasis on the importance of working cooperatively. I suggest to my patients that they concentrate on eliminating as much stress as possible from the their life while I concentrate on removing the effects of stress from their body. Together we can improve overall health as their body begins to function at its fullest capacity and in harmony with them.

We have been conditioned as a society to take a pill to treat the symptom and keep going, instead of slowing down and finding the root cause of why we don't feel well and healing it. Chiropractic care is a holistic approach to treating illness, with the results being longterm and even lifelong. Used in addition to regular medical care or as an alternative therapy, Chiropractic treatments can help you get back in the game of life.

Today, as many as six million Americans have limited mobility due to back, hip, and leg pain, at a yearly cost of over 40 billion dollars in lost work, compensation payments, and medical bills. This is an amazing statistic. Insurance companies have done their part to help by covering some or all Chiropractic care, with little or no out-of-pocket expense to you. It is time to start listening to your body again and take time to heal yourself. No matter what challenges you face in your work, health, or emotional well-being, you can benefit from regular Chiropractic care. Make time for Chiropractic, you deserve it!

Expressing Myself

We continue our journey of healing with a look at our identity. Then we will take steps to express what we find in a way that is personal and fulfilling. Who we feel we are is demonstrated by this self-expression. I say feel because self-expression is a feeling thing. We can know who we are but to be passionate about it, we must be able to feel what we know. The reason we want to be passionate about who we are is because it feeds our desire. Our desire ignites our willingness to express the way we show joy. The way we show joy is our gift. Those around us interpret our gift as our talent. To bring this full circle, we use our talent as an outward demonstration of who we feel we are. I just love circles.

For those of us who have been repressed, this will take a little practice, but is well worth the effort. Repression is a form of denial. The feelings are there, they are just buried deep and more difficult to access. One way to dig up the past and allow old hurts to come out and be released is with a Journal. Some things you may write about are situations and circumstances that caused you to push your true feelings down. You may have done this to protect yourself or to avoid ridicule. You may have done this to yourself or have been repressed by another. Either way, writing about it will help you understand why you lack the desire to express yourself and bring joy back into your life. When writing, include how this made you feel and what you believe about yourself as a result.

As you are writing and remembering, surround yourself with the white light of unconditional love to transmute all negative feelings as they release from you. Also, ask that anyone you are angry with be surrounded and protected by white light while you release your anger at them. If you find that your anger is too great and feelings of revenge arise in you, consult a professional counselor to assist you with this. Whether you choose to work with traditional methods or a spiritual healer, you will need to release the anger in a safe and effective manner. Never limit yourself by being afraid to ask for help.

The key to tapping into real change here is to call upon the power of unconditional love, the source of life, or God to help you liberate the energy locked up by your anger. As this energy is made available, the sensation of lightness and youth will fill you as tension leaves your body. This is personal power, and it is yours to create with.

I use this technique whenever I need help working with my anger instead of suppressing it and later forgetting about it. I learned that the level of personal will that is needed to suppress anger was tremendous and debilitating. It also kept me separated from pieces of myself, leaving me feeling fragmented and without passion for me and my life.

So, after you have gotten out the hurt and pain, and you have come to the neutral place of understanding and forgiveness, you are ready to begin the exploration of who you are and how you want to show yourself to us all.

In my own life, the search for my special purpose began when I was quite young. Growing up with an older sister with notable artistic talent and great beauty, I became acutely aware of my own perceived mediocrity. I remember asking my mother what my talent was, and she told me that I had to find it on my own because it was my own. She gave me a hint though. She told me to look for it in all the things I love to do. She said it could show up in the most unusual places, like when I was playing, attending school, or taking care of my younger sisters and brothers. I began watching out for my talent. Here it is, I thought. It's in the beautiful clothes I made for my doll. No, that's not it, my sister makes better doll clothes than I do. I continued to discover and rediscover my talent in the many art, music, and dancing lessons, but there was always someone better than me, so those couldn't be my talents. I must be an exception. "I'm the only person on the planet without talent," I would lament. No, my mother insisted, everyone has a talent, and it's found when we do the things we love to do. Oh, the things we love to do! Now I know my mother's talent. She helps others find their gifts and talents.

Frankly, I've met people with abundant talent and multiple talents who fuss and fight their gifts. Why do they do that? Are they so dissatisfied with themselves that they can't enjoy the beauty or genius they are creating? I've met others like myself still searching for the action that defines our gifts. Are we so obsessed with being unique or better than everyone that we can't allow ourselves the freeing dance of the soul?

In nature, we see the unbridled expression of the Earth's joy in every leaf and flower. Mother Nature has no judgment on her creations; she just lets them go and be. She allows evolution to create, recreate, and improve on her original concepts, for the sheer joy of experiencing the unlimited ways life can express itself. That same urge is within all of us.

Let this cycle of growth inspire you to throw off the shackles and bring out what is sleeping inside your heart. Just to plant a few seeds; you could sing, paint, write, dance, recite prose, play, or build. Whatever you choose to create, be sure to love it, even if you feel you have to evolve it and recreate it. The process of creation shows you who you are, and you don't have to settle for the first draft. Make sure your foundation is solidly formed in love and appreciation for your gifts. As for me, I found my talent and gifts in being a landscape designer, writer, and healer. By no coincidence, those are the things I love to do.

This month, the month of self-expression you will be introduced to vivacious Deirdra. She is the Goddess of Passion. She will help you find and

continued on page 147

March

Expressing myself

Some Things To Do This Month

Express your feelings as they occur, so they don't get bottled up and blow suddenly like the big winds of March.

Prepare for the changing seasons with grounding exercises to keep you focused and attentive to environmental needs.

Keep your internal organs in tiptop shape especially during times of melancholy and anxiety. Add supplements and exercise to your daily regime.

Living With Moon Energy

The Moon is the closest heavenly body to our planet. Her affect on us is real and immediate. Tracking the phases of the Moon and the zodiac sign she is traveling through can map out a cause and effect cycle for us. It will help make sense of our mood swings and patterns of luck, both good and bad.

Look up the Moon table on page 151 and record the date and zodiac sign the New and Full Moons are in.

Next, write down how you felt the three days around the New and Full Moons. Also record what was happening in your life at these times. Keeping track of this information will help you anticipate and prepare for future influences from the Moon. You may also compare your life with the interpretations provided on page 148.

**Notes on how the energy of the
New Moon and Full Moon affect me.**

March's Goddess

Being passionate about something is like tapping into the fountain of youth. Energy flows through your veins, and your mind is alive with creativity. There is no such thing as no, can't, or never in a million years. All you feel is go, yes, and get out of the way. Passion is such a great high, and the fires within burn brightly. Can't wait to get there? Just call on Deirdra in the meditation below and get ready to feel the burn.

Meditation: To connect with the Goddess of Passion, you will need a handheld drum and drumstick, a candle, and a small table. Place a candle on the small table in the middle of the room. Make sure you have enough space to walk around the table while beating your drum.

Begin your meditation by lighting the candle. While standing, focus on the light in the center of your body. Allow this light to expand and fill your body and aura. Next, imagine a beam of your light extending straight down into the center of the Earth from your tailbone. Then, imagine a beam of your light extending up into the sky from the top of your head. Affirm that this beam is connecting to your source of love. Ask that these beams draw to you love from the Earth and the Source, and fill your body and aura. Feel the space around you becoming safe and loving.

You are now ready to connect with Deirdra. Send a beam of light out to the Goddess of Passion and invite her to bring you her gifts. Begin to softly drum in a pleasing rhythm. As you drum, imagine the energy of the goddess filling your second chakra. It is two inches below your navel. The second chakra is the seat of your creative energy and passion.

As you make the connection with Deirdra, you may feel like swaying or dancing. Allow yourself to be swept away by the beating of the drum and the inspiring essence of Deirdra. Feel the powerful creative energy rise up from your second chakra. Deirdra is helping you activate the emotional impulses needed to fuel your desire for expression. With this flow of energy will come many thoughts, images, and feelings. Just let them bubble up and be in the flow of free association. You are accessing and releasing what has been held there. You may also feel like you are breaking down some walls of resistance. These are the blocks that kept you from tapping into your creative nature. Go with this until you feel complete.

When the energy begins to calm down, slow your drumming to a stop, release Deirdra, and begin to come back into the present by taking a deep breath and stretching. Blow out the candle and write a detailed description of your experience in the March journal pages.

Deirdra *Goddess of Passion*

Feeling alive is what I bring to you. I am passion, and I am more than the feeling of freedom, I am freedom itself. I fly high and far to entice you throw off your inhibitions and show us who you really are.

Even though there is fear in you, and you often speak of love, art, and music as intangible, I still see a desire to create deep within you. Even though I feel your rigidity as you reach inside to find your spirit, there is still a will to break out of your self-imposed prison.

Many of your experiences have trained you to be cautious, and I see you hold your most precious dreams close and almost hidden, even from yourself. I understand that it's just to protect you from rejection. I am here to help you relax and allow your self-expression to flow without regret, guilt, or shame.

Come fly with me in your words, your music, your dance, in your unique way of expressing your truth.

Passion is my gift, and together we can unlock your heart and watch it soar.

"I will weep tears of joy to soften your fortress. My laughter will ignite your desire to feel passion once again."

M A R C H

Draw your heart's desire with a new box of crayons

Expressing myself

Sometimes we do things just because it makes a good story.
What kind of story are you today?

M A R C H

It is upon a dragonfly's flight that imagination is born.
Their shimmering opal wings reflect the depth of what can be.

LightBeings Master Essences - Mastery in Life

By Petra Schneider and Gerhard K. Pieroth

When we began to work with the master energies, we had no idea where it would lead us. In those days, I was very ungrounded. We had lived a completely normal life, and I was done with my studies, referendar training and my position with the Agriculture Chamber. For a few years afterwards, we devoted our time to spiritual work for personal growth and dealt with ethereal energies. Our world revolved around Reiki seminars, seminars for personal growth, and private sessions, and had little to do with the everyday world.

> **"Essence #15, Saint Germain, brings old behavioral patterns and limitations into consciousness and transforms them."**

When the work with the master energies began, I was happy because I only saw the energetic side. Today, I know how much earthly work is connected to it. We are personally involved with every aspect of production and marketing of the LightBeings Master Essences. We handle everything from the energetic work to the bottling to mailing of the packages. Again, I am leading a practical working life - and yet it is not normal. In comparison to before, I am conscious when working.

I found out who I am and try to manifest it in my daily life. I recognize easily what hinders me and has hindered me in the past, and I take steps toward change. For support, I use the essences and the energies of the masters. For example: a few days ago, I again started to work with Essence #15 (Saint Germain). This essence brings old behavioral patterns and limitations into consciousness and transforms them.

Shortly after, I received a phone call from a large store. They had made the decision to take the essences. Actually a reason to rejoice. Yet I was depressed. Suddenly I realized what was the matter. When I looked at it closely, I realized fear and disappointment were there. I recognized that for me, success was connected to the picture: "this is the end, this will be my ruin" - which was complete nonsense, but that's what was there. It also became clear that I have had this pattern for years. Every time a large success showed up, I felt afraid, out of sorts, and had the idea: "this will be the end". The phrase "who climbs high can fall deeply" came to mind. This thought had stopped me when my success got too big. I had never realized this before. Suddenly it was completely clear, triggered by this phone conversation, and now I was able to transform it more easily.

The LightBeings Master Essences work in daily life. Normal life is lived more consciously, and at the same time, blocks are being transformed, and the flow of energy is being strengthened. This leads to the recognition of old patterns and limitations while at the same time we are shown how different our reactions to life could be. Energy is present to transform and help us live this new experience. We become more self-reliant and take life more consciously into our hands.

In seminars, during therapy, and in life's special moments, we often experience our real being. We experience ourselves, our inner strength, liveliness, and the silence. When the experience is over, the effect lasts a few more days before it fades. Then we are back in our daily life with its difficulties, and what was experienced is only a faded memory.

The essences support the work of seminars and therapists because they stabilize and deepen the success of the therapy. When the therapist matches the appropriate essence to the client, blocks to conscious living are transformed. Fears are resolved, and we feel more in charge of our life. We can enjoy ourselves more thoroughly.

What Are LightBeings Master Essences?

The LightBeings Master Essences are a "tool" to experience and live our true being. They are a way to our own mastery. The 21 different essences support the unfolding of life themes like joy of life, love and self-love, inner wisdom, acceptance, inner peace, trust, recognizing your own strength and accepting it,

transformation of the past, action, grounding, truth, intuition.

The essences are available as tincture for taking internally, as oil for external application, and as an energy ball which is worn like a piece of jewelry.

How Do They Work?

The essences affect the aura or the ethereal energy body, through an ethereal vibrational frequency. They dissolve blockages in the mental, emotional, physical, and spiritual energy bodies. They energize, improve the energy flow, and support

---

"They energize, improve the energy flow, and support the body's power for self-healing . . . "

---

the body's power for self-healing, strengthening the connection to our own inner wisdom and higher self. The effective vibration originates from the ascended masters, whose energies are also used by others like Aura Soma and Channels. In regard to the effect of the LightBeings Master Essences on the level of energetic vibrations, they can be compared to Bach Flower Remedies or high-potency homeopathic medicines.

The individual reaction to the essences can vary. Some people feel an effect immediately, like changes in feeling emotions or in the flow of energy. Others experience apparently nothing yet realize, after continuous use for several weeks or months, that they became more open, balanced, and self-confident.

As a reaction to the essences, people also noticed thoughts they did not have before, and were making daily decisions they did not think were possible a short while ago. Old behavior patterns, which accompanied them for a long time, have suddenly disappeared without them being able to tell when this change happened. Sometimes people themselves don't notice the changes that took place because they happen slowly and naturally. Only in hindsight through writing a journal or feedback from friends do they notice their development.

A Few Examples From Experience

A short while ago, a woman using the oils told her experience with essence #10 (Kamakura) which has the theme of "action": "Suddenly I have so much energy, the day cannot be long enough for me, and I get things done with such speed and clarity to which I was not used to."

Another person who used #10 started to tackle all the things he had postponed for a long time. He had known exactly what he wanted to do and what he should do, yet, instead of starting, he lay a long time in bed in the morning and did not feel like starting to do the work. Through #10, he got the drive and strength to do all the work he had put off and finish in a relatively short period of time.

A woman stopped by at the booth we had at the Frankfurt Expo in Germany showing the book and essences. She did not really concentrate on the ongoing dialog. When she drew a card posing the question: "which essence will support me the most in this moment" the theme "Trust" came up (#3 El Morya). When she rubbed a little oil onto her pulse, she instantly noticed how she became calmer, more powerful, and self-confident. Being very enthusiastic about this, she told me she had written a book and actually was supposed to have a discussion with a publisher in half an hour. However, the appointment had been rescheduled, so she walked nervously and anxiously along the booths. In doing so, she had accidentally found the essences. She came back the next day to tell me that her meeting had been successful and that she had felt very calm and centered throughout the whole discussion.

"**When she rubbed a little oil onto her pulse, she instantly noticed how she became calmer, more powerful, and self-confident.**"

The essences also have a positive effect on children, which is shown by the experience of a friend. Her son had started school a short while ago and was suffering from a nervous bladder. This meant he had to go to the bathroom every half hour and was disturbing class as a result. My friend rubbed his belly with oil #3 (El Morya) "Trust" which he enjoyed very much. He would even remind her in case she forgot. After a few days, his condition improved. Now he had to go to the bathroom only every 1.5 hours during the longer classes.

A woman who used essence #19 (Helion) "let your charismatic nature shine" or "Radiance", reported that a few days after the use, other people would approach her in order to work with her, to win her over for new projects, and also offered her money for the projects. Her radiance had become powerful and engaging.

The essences seem to be of help to older people as well. A nurse working in a nursing home recommended them to an elderly woman who was always very restless and sometimes rather confused. A short time after taking the tincture, the woman began to tell about her life and her oppressing experiences. She continued to tell more of her life in the next few days and became calmer and clearer.

What Are Ascended Masters?

Ascended Masters are energy forms or beings of higher consciousness without a physical body who support people with the unfolding of their consciousness. They know about life on earth and about human problems and entanglements and the way to unity. Many of these beings have lived on earth and themselves walked this path of development. Literature can be found about Lao Tse and Kwan Yin. Christ energy can be easily understood through biblical texts. We know from stories that these people traveled the path of enlightenment and evolved to be the masters they are. They experienced the difficulties of human existence and its duality to reach unity again. As they once walked this path themselves, they now support others on their path.

How Did The Master Essences Come About?

Years before I came personally involved with the ascended masters, they fascinated me. When they came into my life in form of the Aura Soma Quintessences, the process began. Through channeling, we received the message that the energy of the masters wanted to manifest again and wanted to bond their energy to matter so they could assist human evolution.

First my mind rebelled: "I can't do this. How could I possibly do this? Maybe others can do it but not I." Yet the message repeated itself, and we got involved in the process. With that, a time of intensive growth and transformation began.

The complete procedure for energizing the preparations, rituals and techniques were channeled to Gerhard and I. We began to manufacture our own essences and work with them. Before we could charge the tincture with the energy of a master, we had to prepare ourselves by clearing our blockages and attuning ourselves to the energy of the master. On a daily basis, we used our charged oils and tinctures and meditated with the energy of the respective master. We channeled and experienced his energy and what it triggered in us. It took between 12 days and 2 months depending on how many blockages we had ourselves to the subject, until we could hold the space for the master. Once we were clear enough, the channeled master came through and bound his energy to oil and water for the production of the essences to be made available to the world.

More than two years have passed since we started to intensively work with the master essences. It has been a time during which we became more and more conscious in being ourselves. Even though there have been difficulties and hard times on this path, in looking back, we realize that we achieved more quality in our life and consciousness very rapidly and unusually easy. We became more authentic, self-confident, livelier, happier, and live more fulfilled. Layer by layer is being transformed and healed, and we are continuing as it is our goal to be fully self-realized.

About the Authors:

Dr. Petra Schneider, born in 1960, studied and received her doctor's degree in the subject of agronomy at the University of Bonn. In 1990, she completed additional training for the teaching profession, administrative work, and consultation, and accepted a position as an official at the Agricultural Chamber. There she dealt with questions related to environmental protection in agriculture and the topics of brown coal and village development. During this time she became intensely interested in the meaning of her life. As a result, she realized that her professional activities didn't provide fulfillment of her life. She quit the secure life-long position and began a deep involvement with subtle energies, meditation, and the possibilities of holistic development of the self. Among other things, one aspect of this was training to become a Reiki teacher, NLP practitioner, and meditation teacher. She now works as a holistic personal

counselor and gives seminars. Since 1994, she has been intensely involved with the energies of the Ascended Masters, resulting in the creation of the Lightbeings Master Essences.

Gerhard K. Pieroth, born in 1956, is a certified industrial engineer and worked for IBM in the production, marketing, and sales departments. As a secondary occupation, he was a lecturer at several institutes of higher learning. In 1988, the failure of his marriage and collapse of his world view led him on the search for meaning in his life and brought him his first experiences with meditation. He opened up increasingly to the abilities he hadn't lived out before that point and quit his job in 1992. Then he trained to be a Reiki teacher and NLP practitioner, among other things. Parallel to this, he trained in the field of adult education and currently works as a holistic success and management consultant, as well as a coach and trainer at companies and for individuals. Together with Petra, he produces the LightBeings Master Essences and holds seminars.

The Lightbeings Master Essences and the Archangels and Earthangels are available through:

High Vibes Distribution
2413 E. Empire St.
Cortez, CO 81321
(800) 339-5106
www.highvibes.org

Spring

March 21st - June 20th
Season of Illumination and Wisdom

We're in the season of quickly changing energy. Life feels more forceful as it pushes outward to begin another cycle. There is a newness that enchants us to believe in great possibilities and make our limiting fears a distant past.

The Eagle is the totem animal of Spring. This high-flying bird is close to spirit, and with its ability to see far and wide, it has great awareness of its surroundings. Soar with this great bird, and tap into spiritual wisdom for answers that guide you through the season of illumination and wisdom. Burn cedar smudge for extra protection while flitting off to loftier realms.

Suggestions for Optimal Seasonal Health

Physical Feeling burned out from doing too much? Feeling scattered from allowing your vital energy to leak out? Practice meditation or get a reiki attunement to learn self-discipline and increase your vital force. See page 61 to learn more about reiki.

Get a physical to make sure all cylinders are firing properly. Consult with your doctor or a nutritionist about taking vitamins and herbal supplements to boost your stamina.

Emotional Keep your enthusiasm charged with the perspective of youth. Make time for playing games, walks in the park, dancing or singing. Observe the world around you as Spring awakens nature, and allow the changes to stir within you, awakening what has been asleep for so long. Let your imagination take a walk on the wild side as you rekindle the joys of childhood.

Mental Energy blockages can develop from stubbornness and unwillingness to work with others cooperatively. Consider seeing someone else's point of view by mirroring their statements. Don't give your opinion until they have completely finished. Allow others' life experiences to touch you. Take a walk in another's shoes for a while. Then you will be able to grasp their unique perspective.

Spiritual Bring illumination to your projects through meditation. Thomas Edison would meditate for long periods of time while he was alone to let inspiration and ideas come to him. It's during the quiet times that our small still voice gives us the answers we are looking for.

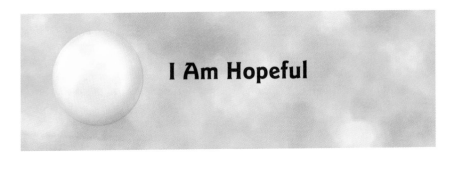

I Am Hopeful

Through failure comes success. I believe this is possible through hope. When I am sitting in my failure and self-pity, feeling like this is truly my darkest hour, much darker than the last one, my mind does an interesting thing. It asks, "What if?" That simple question creates a tiny pinhole of light in my darkness.

"Try not to ignore the quiet questions in your mind. It is hope, and its presence asks you to be open to possibilities and never give up."

"What if?", it repeats, waiting patiently for a response. Of course, my mind has to answer, and then a miracle happens. Rip, tear, and blast, the light of hope floods me, and I consider starting again. Yeah, I'll try it that way or see it another way. Even though I'm not guaranteed success, I am excited again. My willingness to try new things multiplies, and I am full of hope to be successful this time.

What is hope anyway? Where does it come from? Hope is the part of me that doesn't buy into failure. It always believes in me and my resilience. It reminds me of my options, opportunities, strengths, and talents. It is loyal and always on alert, waiting to be of service when I give up. Hope is the light inside of me that speaks to me of how grand I am and delights in my ideas. It's like a parent in awe of its child's process of discovering, experimenting, and learning.

When I allow hope to fill me and inspire me to begin again, I feel renewed. Could this possibly be an act of unconditional love? Wow, I just loved myself. This feels much different than when I sit in meditation affirming that I love myself unconditionally. This is a full spontaneous feeling that puts light in my eyes, a smile on my face, and a tickle in my tummy. I feel like a child again, riding a two-wheel bike without training wheels, and this time I didn't run into the tree.

Try not to ignore the quiet questions in your mind. It is hope, and its presence asks you to be open to possibilities and never give up. Give yourself the chance, you're worth it. And it feels good, too!

I would like you to experience for yourself the action of hope. On the next page, I'll guide you through a creative visualization. Read this through a few times and then put the book down and recreate it in your mind. Keep it light and simple and state your intention to experience hope. If you prefer, you can record it and play it back for yourself.

Remember a time when you were working on a project that broke or failed, and you never went back to it. Recall how you felt. Your face got hot, and your anger boiled up from the pit of your stomach. Thoughts raced through your mind. You remember them, let them come up again. Maybe you cried in your frustration. Let all those emotions flow out of you and gather into a dark mass in front of you. Let this dark mass of anger, failure, disappointment, and hopelessness continue growing until it surrounds you. If you become overwhelmed by the intensity of your emotions, remind yourself that you are just watching, and this is not really happening now.

Now move your attention away from the negative chatter, and ask, in a kind, gentle, and soft voice, "What if?"

Ask again, "What if?"

Give your mind an opportunity to respond. It will create a space for ideas and inspirations if you let it. It will resolve the problem, even if the answer is that there is no solution at this time. Feel the cool calm of hope approaching your awareness. Watch for the pinpoints of light breaking up the darkness of your gloom. Watch them expand and completely overcome the space around you. Beautiful light, hopefulness, and enthusiasm surround you. Feel the joy of mastering your disappointment, and welcome the opportunity to begin again.

If for some reason you remain in the darkness, and the pinholes of light do not materialize, stay in control of your visualization and imagine a bubble of bright white light floating down from above you and surrounding the dark mass you created. Watch as the darkness loses its density and fades quickly into the brilliant light. Feel the intense emotions fade just as quickly, and you are now surrounded only by the white light. Let the white light be the essence of hope for you, filling you with contentment and the knowledge that you will have other opportunities to challenge yourself with your own creations. The exercise is over, and all is back to normal for you with the added benefit of a little more compassion for yourself. There are no mistakes, only experiences. Life is a game, play it well, and play it to learn.

This is the perfect time to introduce our goddess for April. Her name is Monica, and she is the Goddess of Hope. As you have experienced in the exercise above, negative emotions can be overwhelming and trick you into believing you are powerless. Feeling out of control or desperate can be frightening. Participating in Monica's meditation will teach you how to create a place of safety for yourself while you achieve mastery of your mind and emotions.

The featured article for the month of April is about divorce. A funny lady who survived a not-so-funny situation writes about this very personal and painful trial. Her challenge was to get a divorce, get mad and not lose her commitment to being a spiritual person having a human experience. It speaks to anyone who has had to turn the page in their own fairy tale and read the chapters following, "and they lived happily ever after", when their Prince or Princess Charming lost their charm.

April

I am hopeful

Some Things To Do This Month

Harness and control your energy for the intense physical, emotional, and mental activities of Spring with self-discipline through martial arts or meditation.

Find new depth, and pull up leadership qualities from within.

When everything seems to go wrong, seclude yourself, and meditate for clarity.

Living With Moon Energy

The Moon is the closest heavenly body to our planet. Her affect on us is real and immediate. Tracking the phases of the Moon and the zodiac sign she is traveling through can map out a cause and effect cycle for us. It will help make sense of our mood swings and patterns of luck, both good and bad.

Look up the Moon table on page 151 and record the date and zodiac sign the New and Full Moons are in.

Next, write down how you felt the three days around the New and Full Moon . Also record what was happening in your life at these times. Keeping track of this information will help you anticipate and prepare for future influences from the Moon. You may also compare your life with the interpretations provided on page 148.

Notes on how the energy of the New Moon and Full Moon affect me.

April's Goddess

There are countless times in the course of our lives that we lean on the concept of hope to keep us from succumbing to our worst fears. It is a powerful tool that is responsible for inspiring our strength. When we're feeling hopeful, we can perform miracles. Even small miracles change the course of events for the better. It is within our nature to draw on the power of hope. In fact, in desperate times, it can be an involuntary reaction to the stress. During those times, hope is used as an acceptable replacement for denial while we get our emotions back under control and clear out the effects of our fear. Then, we can face our problems, ask for help, or accept the situation knowing that we'll be ok eventually.

Fortunately, we don't have to wait for a crisis. We can solicit the help of our goddess Monica anytime to surround us with her essence and protect us with the reassurance we need.

Meditation: For this meditation, you will need three candles. Sit in a straight backed chair with your feet flat on the floor and the candles on a table near you. Close your eyes and breathe in a slow rhythmic four count pattern. When you feel relaxed, and your mind becomes quiet, return to normal breathing and begin to create your sacred space, as described in February's meditation (page 18).

When you are ready, open your eyes, and light each candle recalling a situation that needs a good dose of hope. The candle to your left represents the past, the candle in the middle is the present, and the candle on your right is the future. Closing your eyes again, imagine a beam of white light extending from your heart into the three flames and invite Monica, Goddess of Hope, to come and make a heart connection with the candles also. Ask Monica to beam hope into the situation and inspiration into your heart. Wait quietly for words, images, or feelings. Or you may ask your questions.

This is your opportunity to get deeply involved with understanding why this happened, what your options are, and what the future may hold. If this is a situation that you just need comforting, let Monica fill you with love and hope. Relax into it and receive. Allow the tears to come and do their part in washing away your pain. Once you feel complete, blow out the candle of the past, closing that door. Next, blow out the candle of the present with better understanding of your situation. Finally, blow out the candle of the future, feeling hopeful. Bless Monica and thank her for the gifts and say goodbye. Call your light back to your center, become fully conscious of your body by moving, stretching, and taking a sip of water. Write your observations in the April journal pages as soon as you are able. Be sure to include images and feelings you may not immediately understand. Reread them later renewed with the calm blessing of hope.

Monica *Goddess of Hope*

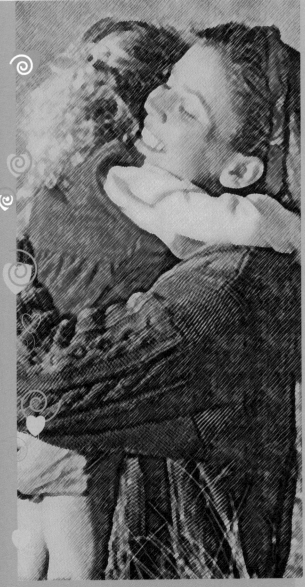

Out of the darkness shines my light. It is a beacon for those of you who have given up hope. My light never fails, even if you fail to see it for a while. I am always here, leading you toward your goal, no matter how hopeless it seems. Allow me to protect you from your wildly destructive emotions and thoughts. I will soothe you and inspire you to stop fighting, calm yourself, and consider beginning again.

Look for me and feel me in places that speak of love and living. I am the sparkle in a child's eye that says, "I believe in you, you can do it." I am the warm embrace that helps you know that you will be loved again. I am the courage you feel that lets you get up and try one more time. I am the wisdom that sets your mind free from limiting thoughts so you can look at life with a fresh perspective.

I am nearest when you feel at the end and truly question your ability to cope. Call me with a desperate cry, a futile whimper, or a resigned sigh. It doesn't matter,
I will hear you.
I will be there.

Don't be afraid. I am here to lead you through your darkest hour. Together, we'll go into the light of hope, and you will make your way.

A p r i l

*The rebirth of spring rejuvenates your spirit with new energy and life,
foretelling the abundance to come in the awakening year.*

I am hopeful

Look beyond the apparent to see life in a new perspective,
full of opportunities to experience universal truth.

A Spiritual Guide To a Graceful Divorce

By Kathy Gabrielle

Falling in love was spectacular; falling out of love has been literally breath-taking. In fact, friends, counselors, doctors, and healers all agree that breathing, although sometimes seemingly optional, is good. Divorce is that blow to your ego, psyche, and most importantly, your heart that takes the breath right out of you, and it becomes your journey to find that breath again and fill your life (and body) with it. How that happens seems to be up for debate.

"Divorce is that blow to your ego, psyche, and most importantly, your heart that takes the breath right out of you."

When I found myself in the middle of divorce, I knew I needed a book. A book would surely give me the answers on how to deal with or possibly even fix the mess that I was in the middle of. What I found were books on legalities, opinions, and sides. There has been a lot written on sides. My side, his side, their side, his new hers side (not my favorite side). I could find books about processing; how to slice, dice, and remove this person from your life. Prayer books, fix or heal you books, what you did to mess up your life and what you can do to find the next one books, but none on how you breathe through

this process books. Now, when you're finding it hard to put one foot in front of the other and in fact find breath, the last thing you want, what I wanted, was to go through a process to heal yourself which at that time seemed worse than the impetus of the journey. What I wanted was to breathe without excruciating pain. So, I kept searching, and I did find pieces that helped. Some were spiritual, some legal, some motivational, but I still searched for the one which said "this is how you get through this process with spiritual values, human emotions including the day to day hurt and still find a way to breathe." So began this journey for me. Following are excerpts from my book in progress that address those things I couldn't find. It is my hope that the following words will bring you peace, a smile, and a good deep breath. Remember, just breathe.

Prince Charming Takes A Hike

I love Cinderella. I love the story. I love the gown, the tiara, and I was always pretty taken with P.C. (Prince Charming). Now in the new age, Cinderella has been given a bum rap. She's been put down as a feminine role model, waiting for someone to come and rescue her from a life of misery. I take great exception to this interpretation. I think she's amazing. She finds inner peace and resolves to be her own person in the middle of a nasty familial experience. She connects daily with nature and animals. She *attracts* to her life what she wants: a life path mate (the newest New Age term for husband) who is loaded, gorgeous, and adores her. I'm missing what's so bad about all of this.

When I met the man I will refer to in this book as "the man formally know as my husband a.k.a. T.M.F.K.A.M.H", I felt he was my P.C. To me, he was gorgeous, fun, and romantic. We shared the same spiritual values or so I thought, had the same outlook on museums (go through and see what you like but definitely skip the tour), and best of all, he said he loved me. We had a whirlwind romance. We went out on a Friday, and by Monday night he said and I quote "I spent all of my life looking for you and now that I found you I never want to be without you again". I was in heaven. I couldn't believe it was really happening to me. Not that I hadn't been working for this moment for as long as I can remember. In fact, I had spent most of the past 33 years preparing for my P.c. by learning about my spiritual path thru creative visualization, affirmative prayer, and holding in thought what you want in your life. To that end, I had even bought my wedding dress. Now, I didn't mean to buy my wedding dress, I was actually looking with a girlfriend for her wedding dress, and I found it. In fact, I thought it a little strange to buy a wedding dress when I wasn't even dating someone. I could however, honestly tell the salesperson, "no date has been set" when she was

going through the list of bridal questions. Talk about an understatement. This, I thought, will show the universe I'm serious about getting married. I'd have a pretty convincing argument when I said I have faith that I'm going to married, and it worked! Almost a year to the day that I bought my dress, I met the man who was to be my husband, and we were married six months later. We lasted five to seven years, depending on how you look at it. The

---

"the man formally known as my husband a.k.a. T.M.F.K.A.M.H. I felt was my P.C."

---

marriage was over in five, but the divorce took another two. I'm surprised by what I remember about our relationship. I still remember some good things like his beautiful blue eyes, his large strong hands, how good he smelled in the cologne I bought for him, and how safe I felt when he held me. I also remember when those beautiful eyes were filled with anger towards me, fear about those large hands hitting me, and how bitter the cologne smelled when he chose to wear it out on dates with his new love while leaving me at home.

New Year's was not even a distant memory when I sensed a change was near. It was mid-February when he he told me he wasn't in love with me anymore, and early June when he said he wanted out, and so began the "Great Release of 97". I remember the day he told me it was over with the same crystal clarity I have for the day he proposed. So, Prince Charming was taking a hike.

I remember feeling the roller coaster of emotions from completely numb to overwhelmed, and as I mentioned earlier, breathing seemed optional at best but mostly just difficult. "What's wrong with me" showed up once or a hundred times, and emotions ranging from rage and anger to the depths of despair were there to be dealt with. I found that divorce grief is much like death grief, only you don't get the life insurance benefits. Thankfully, I was told early on that wanting your spouse dead is as much of a fantasy as believing chocolate is a food group. They are simply feelings that are to be felt and dealt with before they are transmuted into positive, releasable energy.

I had two goals with this divorce. I wanted to get through it so when I was through it, I was through with it. I also wanted it to be amicable. The first I found was a lofty goal, requiring as much dedication and energy as any diet I'd ever tried, and the second was almost as hard as the first. Even from the beginning, help arrived in various packages, and what I have gone through has taught me and helped mold me into the woman I am today. I owe a great deal of my healing to these jewels. I call them the Known Truths.

> No one can hurt you unless you choose to be hurt.

> When the student is ready, the teacher will appear.

I wrestled with these truths the most during my divorce. How could I not be hurt by what was happening? I admit I was the eager student wanting to learn but how could I have brought a teacher in my life that was so completely different than the P.C. I

had envisioned? I remember thinking: if this guy's my teacher, I want a new class!! But alas the Truths held up their truth. Once I caught my breath, I could see for a brief second how he really couldn't hurt me. I was hurt because I would take what he was doing personally. As it turns out, he has been one of the great teachers in my life, and because of this experience I have learned deeper meanings to spiritual trust, release, and surrender. So much for taking the easy courses! Knowing these principles of truthful living and integrating them into the gut-wrenching trials by fire, flood,

---

"The first was a lofty goal, requiring as much dedication as any diet I've tried."

---

avalanche, and famine has been a life saver for me. I not only survived these trials, in fact I'm actually thriving!

As my teacher, he had provided the opportunity for a test run of the beliefs held dear and the new ones learned. Have you ever noticed that when a crisis strikes, you scramble searching through books, tapes, counselors, psychics, ministers, everywhere you can so someone can give you answers? I have sought out all of the above, and they in their own ways provided a "bandaid" for a time. What I have learned, mostly the hard way, is that there is no one outside of yourself that has better answers than you. When you can get still in the middle of the very storm that is rocking you to your core, and listen, really listen to that still small voice, you can't go wrong. It's your never-ending guide through the rough waters, and that is what the departure of my Prince taught me. I desperately wanted to be able to call a friend or a prayer line and have somebody fix my indescribable wound. I needed someone to take the pain away, if only for a little while, so I could catch my breath. Relief did come but only when I did it myself, in meditation, in prayer, and not surprisingly, in breath work. When I took the time to actively calm the chatter, or what I call squirrel caging in my mind, I knew relief. The most noticeable and longest lasting relief appeared after I heard the following story. Remember I mentioned those teachers appearing? One of mine was Ms. Carolyn Myss, author of Energy Anatomy. She is an incredible teacher that has had a lifelong positive effect on many peoples' lives, including my own. One early fall morning, while attending her seminar, Ms. Myss asked us, the group of students, about people who had hurt us. A few of us shared our wounds and after heart-felt listening, Caroline offered this transformative explanation to us all. It's a story of God speaking to the multitudes of angels in heaven asking for a volunteer to help someone learn a major life lesson. Now this lesson would change that person's life for the better, help them grow spiritually, and positively affect them for the rest of their life. The problem is that in order to learn their lesson at the depth they need to learn it, you will have to betray them big time, hurt them deeper than they have ever been hurt before. But, from the healing of that hurt, they will indeed become a better person.

So in my case the angel, who I came to know as T.M.F.K.A.M.H., raises his hand and says "I'll do it. I love her so much that I'm willing to betray her so that she can learn what she needs to learn. I love her that dearly."

It is a powerful story that still affects me today as much as the first time I heard it. Now when you think of the person who has hurt you in these terms, as loving you so deeply and completely that they are willing to play the bad guy in your life, then the

---

"What we are here to remember is that no matter what happens we are not alone . . . We are always guided, and divine protection never stops."

---

whole circumstance takes on a different meaning. When you see the love that is exchanged between the two of you, then forgiveness is possible, and healing is natural. I truly believe that it is at this level where our spirits are set free to be the loving and magnificent beings we really are. What happens is that our ego gets in the way and holds on to being wronged or hurt. Often when we get hurt, we want to give that hurt back, which is always a bad choice. Revenge never leads to anywhere except to more revenge. It takes on a life of its own and goes forth and multiplies. That doesn't mean you just sit back and take whatever is dished out. What it means is that you empower yourself with the only real power there is, your spiritual power.

How many times do we give our power away? We give it to a husband, wife, boss, cop, person next to us on the highway, or even our kids.

It's almost second nature to a lot of us. What these trials teach us is that when we are centered, strong, and sure of our connection to a higher power, God, Universe, whatever you call it, it's in that moment when the divine lesson comes through, and our spirit graduates to a new, higher level. What we're here to remember is that no matter what happens we are not alone. It doesn't matter what test is slapping us upside the head or who walks out of our lives. The truth is that we are never alone, we are always guided, and divine protection never stops. Knowing and feeling this was the foundation of my healing.

What else did I do? Well, I cried a lot, which was also very healing. I stayed busy, and I became even more determined that no matter what the circumstances, I was going to be "*Spiritual*". In my decision to be this pillar of spiritual strength, I forgot one itsy bitsy detail. I was a spiritual being having a human experience. It's the human part that I kind of forgot about. I was so busy seeing *him* as this wonderful divinely-sent teacher that I completely disregarded my human emotions. Not a good idea. Eventually, the pillar collapsed, and I got to feel all those emotions seemingly at once. It felt like I was giving birth to twelve watermelons at the same time; in other words, it hurt!! I was counseled to "feel the stuffing" out of my feelings, remembering to breathe, then feel my feelings, and feel my feelings, and feel them some more. Then, after I've felt them as much as I can, go back and see what I haven't felt and feel that.

This takes an enormous amount of energy and commitment. You need a lot of sleep, reliable friends, and the courage to walk through the exact place you don't want to be. Just know that as you walk through this misery, what awaits you on the other side is absolutely incredible. You find yourself waiting there for you, a you that you didn't even know existed, along with the strength, power, resolve, dedication, commitment, and empowerment that fills you, really fills you, allowing you to be the person you want to be.

It is just as imperative to feel your "humanness" as it is to remember your spirituality during this journey to your empowerment. They go hand and hand together, and one won't work without the other, much as the body doesn't work without breath, but combined, they will offer you your greatest strength and your ability to just breathe.

Kathy Gabrielle has been in the psychic field for more than 20 years. She has appeared on radio and television and is well known for her enthusiasm, humor, and insight. Kathy is gifted in psychometry, clairvoyance, and empathic channeling. Her consultations are enjoyable and informative as they guide you toward discovering purpose and meaning in life.

Rise and Shine

I am from Michigan, and May is our first month of in-your-face warmth and green. Those of us who experience the intense temperature swings of the seasons find this time of year an invigorating wake-up call. Being a morning person, I respond well to this, and I can't seem to wipe the smile off my face. My blood starts pumping, and I breathe a little more deeply and thank the heavens I don't have allergies. I wouldn't want anything to spoil my fun. That's just what May is reminding us to do, have fun.

"Every piece I integrate back into the whole of me brings me a step closer to wanting to live my life more fully"

When life gets serious, and we hurt, there has got to be a way to inspire fun living and joyous feelings. Rising and shining is for the soul, too.

Our soul keeps track of all of our experiences, and it can get clogged up with sadness, anger, hurts, and fear. It can also throw off a piece of itself as a reaction to a traumatic experience. It does this in an attempt to shield our conscious memory of it. Our soul makes many sacrifices for the benefit of our personality. This seems to be a necessary activity to help us cope with some of the more serious sides of life. We can heal and reward our soul for all the sacrifices it makes with love and understanding. Bringing joy back to our damaged soul parts and integrating them back into the whole soul is a technique used for many, many generations.

Shamanic work is the process of healing the soul and retrieving soul parts that have become separate and need help coming home to us. Native American Indian Spirituality specializes in soul retrieval, and the benefits are a feeling of wholeness, contentment, and purpose. I have gone looking for my lost soul parts and have helped many of them heal and come home to me. Every piece I integrate back into the whole of me brings me a step closer to wanting to live my life fully. There is less fear in me and more peace. I feel more, dare I say, empowered. I found myself declaring that I wanted to be in the parade instead of watching it pass me by. I began taking more risks and enjoying the challenge instead of dwelling on what could go wrong.

Helping your soul rise and shine in this way can be learned, and you can do it for yourself. Find a qualified counselor trained in soul retrieval who will take you on your own journey and possibly teach you how. It can be the beginning of a feeling of eternal Spring as you call yourself back to you and learn to live free and breathe deep.

Jessica, the Goddess of Careers, graces May's Journaling pages. She is here to demonstrate the value of desiring and needing to accomplish our goals. Jessica will also help you face the fears that naturally come up when you decide to live your life and rely upon yourself. She is also a great support for those times when there is a big change in your life, like moving, starting college, getting married, getting divorced, starting a family, or losing a loved one.

In preparation for her meditation, reflect on the times you really needed to be strong and were afraid you couldn't be, but you were anyway.

Jessica was there. With this knowing in your heart and Jessica's energy available to you, focus on what you desire to happen now and participate in the meditation with confidence.

I chose this month to talk about Reiki because it is another way to calm, to reduce pain, and to restore balance to your body and life. Marcia Goodman-Blair, M.A. gives us a comprehensive history and explanation of Reiki. She also tells what to expect from a Reiki treatment and how to find and select a Reiki practitioner. Reiki is truly for everyone and anyone can be attuned and give Reiki treatments to themselves and others. Wouldn't it be great to soothe a restless child into slumber with a little Reiki! It will calm mom and dad, too. You will find the Reiki article after the May journal pages.

She Wears Flowers

by Jacki Smith

She wears flowers,
They mirror the ones in her soul
Fresh, Fragrant
        Love from the goddess

Look to see the flowers
        in her eyes,
She is a fragile bloom
        willing to be shared
                unable to be picked

Flowers live
        within her breath
Blossoming with every word
        she speaks

The comfort of a
        bed of rose petals
Surrounds your heart
        as she eases
                your mind

The scent of
        Honeysuckle is
left in her wake
The remembrance of
        her gentle touch
                and the smile in
                all she expresses
                        carries you through

Knowing that she wears flowers
        and the flowers REVEL
                in her presence.

May

Rise and Shine

Some Things To Do This Month

Bring balance into your life by adding spiritual lessons to your pursuit of material success.

Put your blood sugar back in balance and treat yeast infections with Acidophilus and a diet change. Eat more veggies and protein, and avoid sugar and carbs for awhile.

Paint a room you visit often blue to increase tranquility and peace.

Living With Moon Energy

The Moon is the closest heavenly body to our planet. Her affect on us is real and immediate. Tracking the phases of the Moon and the zodiac sign she is traveling through can map out a cause and effect cycle for us. It will help make sense of our mood swings and patterns of luck, both good and bad.

Look up the Moon table on page 151 and record the date and zodiac sign the New and Full Moons are in.

Next, write down how you felt the three days around the New and Full Moons. Also record what was happening in your life at these times. Keeping track of this information will help you anticipate and prepare for future influences from the Moon. You may also compare your life with the interpretations provided on page 148.

**Notes on how the energy of the
New Moon and Full Moon affect me.**

May's Goddess

Let's take a look at our jobs. Are they our careers? Sometimes, and many times, not. For many of us, our jobs have become a means to an end. Money. We all understand the need for money, but what is lost here is the need to have a career that speaks of who we are and what we hope to accomplish. I believe our careers can be our lifework, our purpose. There are many workshops that can inspire us and even teach us how to create the job and do the work we love, but many of us don't do it. Or, we try and quit after awhile. What stops us is more than just the lack of time and money, it is our fear. Fear come in sheep's clothing and sets up a long list of reasons why we can't go from job to career. Getting into and past this resistance is a necessary first step to finding and creating our perfect career. Try the following meditation and meet with Jessica for some career counseling. You have nothing to lose but your own resistance.

Meditation: This meditation is an opportunity to ask the questions no one else can help you with. In preparation for this meditation, write down a few questions about your job or career. Or ask for guidance about what stops you from succeeding. Next, light a burgundy candle and sit comfortably with your back straight and feet on the floor.

Begin breathing slowly and deeply. Once you feel relaxed and your mind is quiet, focus on your inner light in the center of your body. Imagine it growing larger and filling you and expanding into the space three feet around you. This is your sacred space, and in it, you are safe and loved. Next, connect with the pure heart of the Earth by sending a cord of your light into the Earth and then connect to your source of love or creator in the same way.

You are now ready to connect with Jessica, the Goddess of Careers. Imagine a bridge of light spanning out from your solar plexus (the area four inches above your navel) to an imaginary city of crystal buildings in the clouds. On this bridge, you notice a man or woman standing there waiting for someone. You notice a piece of paper in their hand. It is an invitation addressed to Jessica. Soon, a beautiful woman joins your representative, and they both cross over the bridge back to you. You will recognize Jessica by her warmth. She has an aura of helpfulness, and upon invitation, her kind eyes can look into your soul. When you are ready, ask your questions and wait quietly for answers. If you have trouble understanding your message, ask that the guidance be revealed to you in a way that you can: a dream, a song on the radio, or a commercial on TV, for example. When you are done, thank Jessica and say goodbye. Watch the bridge dissolve, and bring your attention back into the room, move around a little, and record your message on the May journal pages. If you have a revealing dream in the nights to come, record that also.

Jessica *Goddess of Careers*

I represent the need and drive to identify and participate in your life's work. I look into your soul and reveal to you what it is you want to accomplish this lifetime. I commit my energy to moving you past the inertia of resistance in any form and keep you focused on making the right choices.

I do this by helping you face your fear and overcome the many obstacles that fall before you on your path. As you experience victory over each challenge, you will feel stronger and more confident.

This is how you build your resolve and character, and develop the strength to live and express the person you are through your career or lifework.

Invite me into your innermost dreams, and I will help you recognize the wisdom in your struggles, choices, and experiences. I will help you tap into the stream of consciousness that reveals the deeper purpose of your life and lead you to the perfect way to fulfill it. I am the Goddess of Careers, step into my office, and let's create the ideal one for you.

Every life is precious and worth the effort put into living it. I will help you create a life full of joy and accomplishment.

Jessica **57**

M A Y

*Breathe deeply the gentle hues of Spring and find
sanctuary from the day's stress.*

Rise and shine

Look for miracles in the most unlikely places.
Believing is seeing!

M A Y

The freshness of a dawning day awakens and energizes your spirit.

Reiki: A Safe Way To Restore Balance To Our Lives and Bodies

By Marcia Goodman-Blair, M.A.

How Reiki Began

Reiki is an ancient spiritual healing method, which is thought to have originated in Tibet over 2,500 years ago. About 100 years ago, Mikao Usui, a Japanese teacher and scholar rediscovered Reiki. A Hawaiian woman of Japanese descent, Hawayo Takata, learned Reiki from one of Usui's successors and brought Reiki to the Western world in the late 1930s. Often referred to as "The Usui System

---

"Reiki (ray-key) or Universal Life Force Energy is the name that Dr Usui gave to this form of energy."

---

of Natural Healing", Reiki is practiced worldwide by several million people. Although variations in the way it is taught and practiced have developed over the years, Reiki remains a simple, yet powerful practice, which may be learned and utilized by anyone who is interested in energy healing. Since the philosophy of Reiki states that it works only for the Highest Good, it is a safe, gentle, non-invasive way to restore balance to the system, while reducing the effects of pain, stress, and disease. Although Reiki has a spiritual component, it is not a sect or religion and is compatible with all beliefs. People who have learned Reiki often find themselves becoming more spiritually connected to their own religion or becoming interested in new practices.

Reiki (ray-key) or Universal Life Force Energy is the name that Dr. Usui gave to this form of energy (it may be compared to the Eastern concepts of Chi or Prana). The ability to channel this energy is activated by a series of attunements passed by a Reiki Master to his or her students. The attunement process allows the energy to flow through the practitioner's hands and into the energy field of the receiver, releasing energy blockages that may contribute to stress or illness.

This process of opening to the energy may be compared to turning on a light switch. Reiki energy promotes the natural ability of an organism to heal and repair itself.

Reiki Training

Traditionally, Reiki training is divided into three or four levels. At Level I, the student learns the history and philosophy of Reiki, along with the hand positions for treating the self and others. In Reiki II, advanced techniques such as distant healing, mental/emotional balancing, and sending Reiki to help heal world situations are learned. Three healing symbols are given at this level to bring additional focus and intent to the student's work. The Master level, Reiki III, may be offered as a complete training or divided into two parts, Master Practitioner and Master Teacher. At the Master level, the student has generally been working with Reiki for personal healing as well as giving treatments to others for some time.

Reiki Treatments

During a typical Reiki session, the recipient lies fully clothed (after removing shoes) on a comfortable bodywork table or may be seated in a chair. The room is usually warm and quiet, the lighting is dimmed, and soft music may be playing in the background. A complete treatment usually takes about an hour. As the practitioner channels the Reiki, the recipient may be aware of the energy moving through his or her body. A sense of peace and deep relaxation is experienced, and often warmth as well as tingling or vibration is felt in the areas being treated. Reiki works to balance the physical, mental, emotional and spiritual levels, thus enhancing well-being and assisting the receiver's healing process.

Some Forms of Healing Addressed by Reiki

- Reduction of stress-related symptoms.

- Greater insight into life situations.

- Enhancement of personal and spiritual development.

- Release of energy blockages that produce disease and discomfort.

- Release of habits or thought patterns which no longer serve the individual.

Reiki is wonderful for treating pets and other animals, too. They usually respond quickly to the energy; it feels as calming and healing for them as it does for humans. It also may be used on plants and to "clear" the energy in a room.

> "A sense of peace and deep relaxation is experienced, and often warmth as well as tingling or vibration is felt in the areas being treated"

People in many different professions and life situations are drawn to Reiki. Some use it primarily for friends and family, while others choose to make it a more professional practice. Nurses, massage therapists, and social workers often take Reiki training, but it can benefit anyone from kindergarten teachers to computer programmers. Some medical schools now offer Reiki as an elective course.

Reiki easily complements the more conventional medical methods. Because of its gentle, non-invasive nature, Reiki enhances all forms of health care. However, it is never a substitute for medical treatment. Reiki encourages people to take a more active role in their own wellness.

Finding a Reiki Master or Practitioner

Once a person decides to experience a Reiki treatment or take Reiki training, how do they go about finding the right Master Teacher/Practitioner to work with? One of the best ways is personal recommendation by a friend or someone whose opinion you respect. In many areas of the US, there are local so-called New Age publications (in my area of New England, some of these are: *Spirit of Change*, *Earthstar* and *Sacred Pathways*) which are often available free of charge at bookstores, coffee shops, and natural food stores. These have listings and advertisements by various practitioners, and most have a section specifically for Reiki or Energy Healing. The Internet is another good source of Reiki information. Two helpful websites are: www.iarp.org (The International Association of Reiki Professionals) and www.reiki.org (The Center For Reiki Training).

After you have found the names of several Reiki practitioners in your area, you are ready to choose one. Some Masters offer Reiki clinics or circles, which are open to the public for a small donation and are often held at holistic centers, churches, metaphysical shops, and bookstores. This is a good place to try a treatment, meet Reiki practitioners in person, and have some of your questions answered. In looking for a teacher or practitioner, some good questions to ask are:

- How long have you been teaching or practicing Reiki?

- What is your understanding of the healing process?

- What other alternatives (massage therapy, Polarity, etc.) do you practice?

- How can Reiki help me heal and/or grow?

- What do you charge for a treatment or class? (Fees vary greatly, so ask a few practitioners to find out the going rates in your area.)

There are also many good books about Reiki available at your local library or bookstore. Many of these have been written in the past few years, as new information about Reiki has been brought to light.

Reiki brings more joy and peace to the lives of those who choose to follow its path. May it bring to you, too, that inner light and harmony that is one of its greatest blessings!

My healing practice integrates the many aspects of healing, spiritual practice, and astrological knowledge that I have studied and worked with for over 25 years. With a Masters Degree in Psychological Counseling and certifications as an Energy and Crystal Healer, as well as extensive Astrological Studies, I offer healing and learning experiences for those who wish to explore alternative paths to holistic well-being.

I am available for energy healing sessions and astrological consultations in Massachusetts and New Hampshire and also teach classes and workshops throughout the New England area. For more information or to receive a current workshop and Reiki class schedule, please call, visit or write:
Marcia Goodman-Blair, M.A.
Reiki Master Teacher
Certified Crystal/Energy Healer
Astrological Counselor

603-382-4725

www.soulpatterns.com

Soul Spirit Journey
The Lyman Center
58 Macy Street
Amebury, MA 01913

Mikao Usui & Reiki

Mikao Usui was the principal of a Christian monastery in Kyoto, Japan. Upon the request of his students, Usui left his position at the seminary in search of the elusive healing techniques used by Jesus.

Legend states that he went to America and studied theology at the University of Chicago. However, he could not find any answers in Christian writings regarding hands-on healing. Returning home to Japan empty-handed, Usui moved his attention to the old Buddist sutras and discovered ancient sanskrit formulas and symbols. These seemed to hold the answers he was looking for.

At the time of his find, he decided to travel to the holy mountains of Kuri Yama to fast and meditate. He stayed in solitude for 21 days in hopes of gaining contact with a higher consciousness which was described in the sanskrit formulas. On the 21st day, he saw a shining light moving toward him at great speed. It became larger and larger until it finally hit him in the center of his forehead. He saw millions of colored bubbles spanning the entire rainbow and more. A great white light appeared, and he saw the sanskrit symbols in front of him glowing in gold. This was the birth of the Usui system of Reiki as revealed to him by the Buddist sutras.

The Three Healing Miracles

On his way down the mountain, Usui tripped and fell, cutting his toe on a rock. His toe was bleeding and very painful. Usui instinctually grabbed his toe with both hands. The bleeding stopped, and the pain disappeared.

That was the first miracle.

Coming upon an inn, Usui decided to stop and eat. He was very hungry after his fast. Even though he was warned by the innkeeper not to eat so much, Usui consumed his entire meal without any discomfort. That was the second miracle.

After watching Usui for a period, the granddaughter of the innkeeper approached him for help. She had been suffering from a toothache for days and was in a lot of pain. Usui put his hands on her face, and her pain subsided immediately. That was the third miracle.

After a few years in the monastery, working with the Reiki energy with his students, Usui decided to go out to the villages and help the poor lead better lives. It didn't take long for Usui to notice that he was seeing the same faces return repeatedly for healings.

When asked why they hadn't begun a new life, the poor stated that it was easier to go on begging than work for a living and be responsible for themselves.

This deeply troubled Usui, and in his grief, he composed the Ethical Principles of Reiki. He wanted to teach the poor about gratitude in hopes that it would inspire them to choose a better life.

Just for today, do not worry.
Just for today, do not anger.
Honor your parents, teachers and elders.
Earn your living honestly.
Show gratitude to everything.

Mikao Usui taught eighteen Reiki Masters before his death in 1930. We are all grateful for his discovery.

This article is compiled from a variety of sources.

Sowing New Seeds

I'm not a farmer, but something within me is compelled to honor the cycle of beginning, middle, and end. As you are beginning this month, you will find yourself in the middle of our seasonal cycle, and I can't help myself from leading you down the path to the pastures and gardens of your mind. Here, with hands full of seed ideas, we will plant them all with great anticipation for a bright and bountiful future.

"This is junk food for the soul that saps your enthusiasm for life. "

This metaphor demonstrates the lesson that what we do today affects our future. Just try to explain that to a teenager. Living for the moment is their plan, and a beautiful one at that, but there is a lesson here as well. In the moment, plant some seeds for your future. Be conscious of which seeds you plant. There is a lot of unconscious farming going on out there. That negative self-talk can take root, too.

How disappointing to come to your garden ready to harvest abundance, joy, peace, and fulfillment only to come up with a handful of I can't, I won't, I'm stupid, what's the use, it won't work out. This is junk food for the soul, and a steady diet of that saps your energy and enthusiasm for life.

Fortunately, the growing season is long and forgiving. You will get

another chance to plant your winter crops. This time, separate the weed seeds out by finding out what your doubts and fears are, and heal them. Allow your doubts and fears to come to your consciousness through meditation, or write about them in the journal pages. No matter what technique you use, the subconscious beliefs have to be revealed in order for you to learn why you are discouraged. Only then will you be armed with the awareness needed to correct those beliefs and let them go.

I tried tossing my "weed seeds" aside, but I got the same results as I did with making New Year resolutions as a child. It just goes to show you can't fake healing. I have a note on my refrigerator to remind me of the danger of this logic. "Doing the same thing over and over and expecting different results is the action of an insane person." To avoid that pitfall, I had to make changes, real changes. I had to be honest with myself. When I hurt, I had to admit it. When someone wasn't good for me, I had to say so, and sometimes I had to say goodbye. I had to look up the definition for co-dependent and then look in the mirror and confess that I had tendencies toward that, too. Then I had to learn why I did that and learn how to be with people in a different and healthier way. I had to correct my behavior by valuing myself as much as I valued others, but that's for another chapter. I was feeling humiliated, lost, and awkward in my own life. It was darn weird, but I found myself in the process.

Possibly the most difficult thing to change was myself. My whole identity was invested in who I thought I was. Letting go of that took determination and patience. I'm not the rip and tear sort of person when it comes to personal change. It has to be gradual and inspired, or I hold on all the tighter.

Incredibly enough, a single nagging thought persisted, and I heard it. "Patty, you are not this weak and sad", it whispered to me. "Oh my God, one seed of desire survived the onslaught of weeds of negativity," I exclaimed. It was just the inspiration I needed. I had to nurture this thought. It needed a lot of attention, and I had to be dedicated to its survival. This one thought or desire was going to be my anchor as I began my journey to better emotional and mental health.

That's how this phase of my evolution began, and I continue with lots of help and support from friends, family, professionals, and spirit. We come into this world with great potential, and I'm getting in touch with mine again. Like all new converts, I'm excited about the changes I've made in my life and the results I've gotten. I want to open doors for anyone who asks. That small quiet desire that wanted me to realize my strength and joy grew up to be this Healer's Almanac.

You have the same potential within you, and I understand the courage and dedication it will take to choose to let it grow and mature.

Of all the Goddesses available to be a guide and hold the door open for you, I chose Kathleen. She is the Goddess of Gardening, and with her meditation, she will gently wash away your fear, anger, and sadness. She will hold your heart safe as you strive to recreate your life in your own way and in your own time. Invite Kathleen into your life for some good old-fashioned nurturing.

This month, we will look at three very effective ways we can use to support the new choices we make to change and improve our lives. Cranio Sacral Therapy, and Radix Feeling and Purpose Bodywork are both presented by Ellen Baker Costantino. Ellen graduated from the Upledger Institute where Cranio Sacral Therapy was developed. She has over ten years of experience and a private practice in Caledonia, Michigan. Ellen shares with us what Cranio Sacral Therapy and Radix are, how they work, and how they can benefit us in easy-to-understand language.

Pat Donovan approaches growth, choice, and change with a more spiritual influence. In her article "Redesigning Our Lives with Channeled Wisdom", Pat presents us with her talent for bringing guidance from a more heavenly perspective. Backed by her own understanding of health, life, and getting through the blockages to happiness, Pat provides an opportunity to get in touch with ourselves on a much deeper level. The channeled information from the collective consciousness is personal, accurate, and very healing. I have had many sessions with Pat, and I have found them to be informative, uplifting, and a lot of fun. Afterward, I felt calmer and it was easier to make the changes I needed to make.

June

Sowing New Seeds

Some Things To Do This Month

Spend time in nature, taking up its beauty through your senses to uplift your spirit.

Let the energy of this month help you focus on initiating projects.

Investigate the healing benefits of yarrow (achilles millefolium). It's used as a tonic and strengthens your immune system, especially when battling the cold or flu.

Living With Moon Energy

The Moon is the closest heavenly body to our planet. Her affect on us is real and immediate. Tracking the phases of the Moon and the zodiac sign she is traveling through can map out a cause and effect cycle for us. It will help make sense of our mood swings and patterns of luck, both good and bad.

Look up the Moon table on page 151 and record the date and zodiac sign the New and Full Moons are in.

Next, write down how you felt the three days around the New and Full Moons. Also record what was happening in your life at these times. Keeping track of this information will help you anticipate and prepare for future influences from the Moon. You may also compare your life with the interpretations provided on page 148.

**Notes on how the energy of the
New Moon and Full Moon affect me.**

June's Goddess

Looking at our soul as if it were a garden is a way of demonstrating that the soul is a living and growing part of us. Our soul actually reflects back to us our experiences, attitudes, and beliefs, and the reflection changes as we change. It can appear withered and lifeless through neglect and abuse. Just like tending a garden renders beautiful results, taking care of ourselves on the soul level polishes our outward life. There are many ways to tend to your soul's development. One way is to become a proficient gardener of the soul. To get started, we will learn from the Goddess of Gardening herself, Kathleen. When you meet her, she will feel like the Earth Mother, full of joy, strength, and a contagious vitality.

Meditation: For this meditation, you will need a green candle, a straight backed chair, and a private place. Start by lighting your candle and stating your intention, "It's time to visit the garden of my soul and ask Kathleen, the Goddess of Gardening to help me". Close your eyes and begin breathing deeply and slowly until you feel relaxed. Focus on your intention.

Imagine roots growing from your feet and tailbone. Watch them grow deep and connect to the heart of the Earth. Then, notice branches growing upward from your head and arms. Watch them grow high and wide. With each breath, you notice light rising up from the Earth and flowing down from the heavens. This light fills you and overflows into the space around you. You are now in your sacred space and ready to go to your garden.

Focus your attention on your heart. Now, go deeper into the center of your heart. Notice a set of doors. Reach out and open them, and step into your garden. Don't judge the space, just observe it. Make some mental notes about what you find there and how you feel about it. Does something look out of place or unhealthy? Later, record these elements in your journal.

As you look around, you notice an older yet vital woman standing in the center of your garden. She is smiling at you, and you immediately know who she is. It's Kathleen. You walk toward each other and greet each other warmly. Hand in hand, you walk around the garden together, discussing its condition and begin forming a plan. Take your time and listen to Kathleen's input. Ask questions when you don't understand, and remember that this is a work in progress. You will not be expected to get everything done this visit, so don't allow yourself to become overwhelmed.

Now, ask Kathleen for a healing. Let everything than can be done in this visit be done, and feel lighter and happier for it. Thank Kathleen for her gifts, say goodbye, and make plans to meet again. See yourself closing the garden gate, and return your attention to the room, stretch, and blow out the candle. Once you feel alert, write about your experience on the journal pages with as much detail as possible.

Kathleen

Goddess of Gardening

There are many gardens to attend to, and the most important one is the garden in your soul. I am Kathleen, the Goddess of Gardening, and I am here to bring you back to yours.

Within each one of you is a place where you grow your life. It is the one garden that you must never neglect. When you do, well, life just seems to become more difficult for you.

The way to your garden is an easy one, but the work begins once you get there. If you haven't been to your garden in a long time, it may be overgrown with hurt, dark and overcast with hopelessness, or dry and barren with hatred. Don't be afraid, these conditions are temporary and easily fixed with a little attention and a lot of love.

Like all good gardeners, I have effective tools to use. They are patience, humor, kindness, strength, optimism, protectiveness, and discernment. All of these tools are essential to ensure a healthy and enthusiastic life, especially in stormy times. Now, lets get started.

"I have never been to a garden I couldn't mend. Let me tend to your garden, and together, we will create a paradise."

J U N E

The seeds of magic are found in your imagination
and planted in your deeds.

Sowing new seeds

Drop a penny today. Let it bring luck to a stranger.

Healing Our Lives With Channeled Wisdom

By Pat Donovan

We are all fortunate to be living in a world where there are so many choices available in the healing profession. Whether one is looking to maximize their body, release emotional baggage, or tap into spiritual awareness, there is an almost limitless amount of practitioners to choose from. The most important thing is to decide what it is you are looking to accomplish, and then find the healer that best suits your needs. I also encourage blending more than one healing practice for the most beneficial outcome.

I am a spiritual counselor who incorporates intuition along with channeled information to assist each client. My intent is not to heal, but rather to redesign the whole person. This is accomplished by my background in human potential, coupled with a high level of empathy and opening up to Source. This formula allows me to step aside while the stream of spiritual consciousness flows through. The information is much more than data; it is an exchange of energy that brings tremendous comfort.

I have witnessed countless individuals who, after only one or two sessions, were able to restructure their lives to a better place. I share through meditation what I receive energetically about the person, then walk them through the process of opening up to spirit. As each individual creates a space to receive, insight and probability patterns will be cast onto them to digest and assimilate. There is a blending of information regarding past, present, and future, as well as a complete scanning of the physicality. The only requirement from the client is the desire for change.

"I have witnessed countless individuals, who, after only one or two sessions, were able to restructure their lives to a better place "

The sessions can be done by phone, in person, or even in a group dynamic. Whenever I am asked what the sessions are like, I find it difficult to articulate, as they are very experiential and unique to each person. What I offer is yet another path on the journey to empowerment.

You can reach Pat Donovan for a consultation at:
Talisman Consulting
(928) 468-1078
www.talismanconsultingintl.com

Cranio Sacral and Radix

By Ellen Baker Costantino

In this new Millennium, we are awakening to the fact that being "healthy" means considering our emotional, mental, and spiritual being as well as our physical being. We know now that just treating physical symptoms medically, without knowing and healing their underlying causes, rarely results in regaining our full health and vitality. Even though conventional medicine still has some uses for us, now we turn more frequently to holistic methods of

---

"I have experienced many forms of bodywork in the last 20 years, and two were particularly effective in helping me heal my physical and emotional health crisis"

---

treatment in order to recover and maintain our health. Fortunately, today we have available to us an array of highly effective and proven methods of healing such as chiropractic, massage, acupuncture, and many other forms of good bodywork.

I have experienced many forms of bodywork in the last 20 years, and two were particularly effective in helping me heal my physical and emotional health crises. Because they

have been so helpful to me on my own healing path, in this article I will share these with you in the hope that they will serve you as well as they have served me in gaining the life I wanted.

The two methods I have been using since 1984, and practicing since 1991, are called Radix Education in Feeling and Purpose, and Cranio Sacral Therapy. It is my deepest desire that you find those methods that bring you to your greatest health and vitality in this life, and I encourage you to explore what these methods have to offer you.

Cranio Sacral Therapy: What Is It?

The Cranio Sacral system consists of the many membranes, bones, and cerebrospinal fluid that surrounds and protects the brain and spinal cord. It extends from the top of the skull bones (cranium) all the way down to the tailbone (sacrum). Like other systems in the body, this system has its own unique rhythm. Normally the brain's fluid flows at a rate of 6-12 cycles per minute as it travels from the brain to the sacrum and back again without resistance. But during disease or injury, the membranes carrying the fluids may become damaged, limiting the normal fluid flow and nutrition to nerve trunks along the spine. A host of physical ailments can follow when fluid flow is thus restricted from nourishing the core nerves of the body. Cranio Sacral Therapy gently balances and restores the normal fluid flow and pressure to the brain and spinal cord. Optimal health and vitality follow when the brain and its nerves are fully nourished and move freely.

How Does It Work?

Cranio Sacral Therapy (CST) was developed 25 years ago by Dr. John Upledger at Michigan State University to heal injured tissues, treat chronic pain, and heal headaches, infections, and a host of other ailments. Because of its positive influence on the central and autonomic nervous systems, CST heals a wide variety of body ailments. Therefore, CST is practiced today by many healthcare professionals including Osteopaths, Dentists, Physical Therapists, Occupational Therapists, Acupuncturists, Massage Therapists, and licensed body workers. The healing effects of CST are a result of two natural forces being used together.

The first is the client's own natural body intelligence that guides his healing process.

The second is the therapist's light hands-on energy that assists the client's hydraulic forces in regaining normal function.

Since CST works with the body's natural healing mechanisms to improve the functioning of your brain and spinal cord, stress on your whole body is decreased, and overall health, vitality, and resistance to disease are increased.

CST is a gentle technique that uses light touch to follow, diagnose, and adjust the CS rhythm. Therapists can palpate the CS rhythm anywhere on the body.

Once the injuries are located, treatment is conducted as the therapist lightly assists the release of restrictions so that the Life Force can flow freely once more. A normal session takes about one hour with the client sitting or lying down. Results are most often seen by the end of the session or within a few hours of treatment.

"Because of its positive influence on the central nervous system, CST heals a wide variety of body ailments."

Is It Safe?

Both physicians and body workers have used CST in this country for over 20 years. Because it is a non-invasive, non-chemical, natural treatment, there are no negative side effects to worry about. CST is safe enough to use with children of all ages, with infants, and even with pregnant women. The following conditions have responded well to CST:

Infections, fevers, sprains, strains, chronic pain, depression, anxiety, ear and eye problems, scoliosis, small strokes, allergies, autism, spastic CP, headaches, TMJ pain, digestive disorders, injuries, trauma, learning disabilities, endocrine imbalances, and even longstanding psychological or character issues from childhood.

Radix Education in Feeling and Purpose Bodywork

This therapy's focus is more on personal growth and psychological healing, so this form of bodywork is best suited to adults and is usually not used with children.

In the first half of this century, Dr. Wilhelm Reich discovered an important relationship between body processes and emotional functioning that were critical to the current holistic health movement. He was ahead of his time in understanding the relationship between emotional stagnation and physical disease.

At the root of this emotional stagnation was emotional armor or chronic tension in the muscles and other tissues blocking the natural flow of feelings/emotions through the body. Reich learned that working directly with tissues and breathing patterns helped people to release blocked feeling. Energy was able to flow through the body normally again, leaving a person more alive, in better health, and in better contact with themselves and others.

Radix is an educational process, which promotes the integration of mind and body, helping us to experience our Real Selves. It combines teaching, psychological processes, physical exercises, soft energy work, communication, and body awareness training to facilitate personal growth and insight, as well as better physical functioning.

The goal of Radix work is to experience and integrate feelings in balance with thinking. Each person is supported in learning to take healthy control of his/her own life, constructing and maintaining boundaries needed to build and sustain higher levels of energy for fuller living.

It has been well-demonstrated that our emotions create physical changes. For example, fear can cause heart palpitations, and anger can cause high blood pressure and stroke. Abdominal problems, arthritis, asthma, hives, and respiratory problems have all been related to psychosomatic responses. Some

---

"Reich learned that working directly with tissues and breathing patterns helped people to release blocked feeling."

---

cancer studies have shown that fear, hate, and guilt underlie cancer development. People suffering from depression are known to recover faster with physical therapies than by any type of psychotherapy alone. Psychosomatic illnesses result from long-term internal stress brought about by repression (blocking) of unacceptable feelings, and this has been known for over 30 years. Radix helps people release their emotional repression and restores the normal, healthy integration of mind and body with which we were born.

Emotional blocking begins in the early years of childhood. Infants need the warmth and touch of loving caretakers to encourage and support their development. They also need freedom to risk, explore, and be spontaneous. But for many children, the free expression of feelings is denied or punished, so they learn to hide or deny their feelings in order to survive in the family and culture. The Real Self, full of vitality, creativity, and aliveness, is often not allowed to emerge.

When natural expression is punished, children learn ways to block expression of those feelings to survive. For example, if a parent threatens "If you don't stop crying, I'll give you something to cry about," the child learns to hold his breath, tighten his jaw, tighten his chest, and choke down his throat feelings and sounds to hide his anger and fear. Over time, this pattern of holding and blocking becomes unconscious, chronically preventing emotional expression. Worse, the emotional armor developed to block "negative" emotions ends up limiting or blocking our positive emotions, because feeling pathways in our bodies are similar for both "good" and "bad" feelings.

For some, the blocks are more damaging than for others, but for all of us, the price we pay is a loss of aliveness and vitality. Over time, we become dull, deadened, and estranged from others and ourselves. When an experience is very painful or traumatic, and we do not get to work through that experience in a safe way, the feelings are blocked from our awareness to protect us, but they are stored in our bodies. In a very real sense then, our bodies are the "unconscious". This information becomes disowned and unavailable on the conscious levels. We continue to be confused and limited unconsciously because thinking and feeling have become split.

Radix work seeks to bridge the gap between thinking (mind) and feeling (body) by slowly loosening armor so blocked feelings and memories can re-emerge and be processed in a safe setting. Once they are fully experienced, we have choice about surrendering to emotions or containing them until another time rather than reacting inappropriately. At the same time, we can choose to let go of thinking at times and just enjoy our positive feelings in life. Life flows smoothly when we return to a balance.

"Radix work seeks to bridge the gap between thinking and feeling by slowly loosening the armor, so, blocked feelings can emerge safely"

If you are interested in further information on either of these methods or would like to set up an initial appointment with a half-off discount, you may contact me.

Ellen Costantino
10422 Alaska Ave. S.E.,
Caledonia MI, 49316
Phone 1-616-891-7578
Fax 1-616-891-7579
Email : "EBCostantino@earthlink.net"

A Woman . . . Alone

By Jacki Smith
Fireball rising
    Tuning the mornings glow
        to the melody of days beginning
A woman alone
    Contemplating her journey
        through life's mysteries
Who is she?
What destiny does she follow?
Who laid out the map?

Summer

June 21st - September 20th

Season of Growth and Trust

As we enter the season of growth, the purpose of our lives becomes clear, and we put our plans into action. Now is the time to trust our feelings and instincts to choose the correct path and let the others fall away. The energy of this season is about using all the wisdom gained from past experiences, and the experiences of those who have gone before us, to create a legacy of our own. It may be a family, a project, or a work of art. Whatever it may be, this is now the time to let it mature.

The trickster Coyote is the totem animal of Summer. Trust the Coyote to trick you out of the ruts of inflexibility and learn your lessons. Let laughter coax you out past your limiting self-talk. Smudge with tobacco to enhance communication with spirit when seeking guidance.

Suggestions for Optimal Seasonal Health

Physical Soothe muscle pulls from overexertion with homeopathic Arnica cream, alternating heat and cold, and white willow bark herbal supplement for pain relief (as long as you're not allergic to aspirin). Take serious action against those allergies with a visit to the CST practitioner for Cranio Sacral Therapy.

Emotional Clear blockages created by your fear of success with Inner Child work. During meditation, find your inner child and give it your unconditional love. Help it heal the wounds of your childhood and become your own loving parent. Promise to spend time with it on a regular basis by taking yourself to the park, buying yourself an occasional treat, and just playing. Joy is the essence of your inner child, so the more you bring joy into your life, the healthier both you and your inner child will be.

Mental Believe you are part of a great process and contribute to it with your gifts. Let this season of growth and trust inspire you to identify and develop your talents. Coming out with a grand version of yourself is just what the mind needs for stimulation.

Spiritual Develop your intuition and use it responsibly for the betterment of the whole world. Your soul desires to be of service to humanity, and it holds the key to your own personal expression of this. Relax, go within, and discover the beautiful mark you want to place on the world.

Letting My Light Shine

"**O**h, what a glorious child of God you are." That's what they told me in church. When I was quite young, it was easy to believe. I felt it too, and I was happy just to be me. As I grew older and continued to embarrass myself and frustrate my parents, I began to seriously consider that I belonged on the outside of the Glorious Child of God Club, destined to be looking in. It wasn't until I learned the expanded version of forgiveness that I could feel my light begin to shine again. Don't throw the book against the wall, I'm not going to hold out on you. The secret to forgiveness is that there is nothing to forgive. In other words, there is no sin. Good or bad, right or wrong, God cherishes all of our experiences. Much is learned by our "playing".

Think of life as an opportunity to experiment with ideas, concepts, and cause-and-effect scenarios. The people in our lives are here to help us act out these trials. We could be teaching ourselves a personal lesson or bringing in a new technology for all of humanity. We may also be here to help someone else learn something and acting a role in their play. A mistake can be viewed as an experiment with an undesirable outcome for yourself or another. Even though this information can be liberating, it doesn't reduce the emotional impact, and it can still affect our belief system. When we get hurt, it's a shock to our system, and everything within us goes into action to put it right. It's our already established feelings, beliefs, and values that cause us to be judgmental and create this need to react.

At this point, we have a choice. We could choose to experiment with violence, revenge, repression, and other self-destructive behaviors, or we could respond with compassion, love,

> "It wasn't until I learned the expanded version of forgiveness that I could feel my light begin to shine again"

and understanding. The complicated web of karma begins in this way, and we have set it up as a universal law to help us learn. This synchronistic dance of life bouncing off life is the perfect platform for teaching us how our actions touch others like overlapping ripples caused by stones thrown in a pond.

By definition, karma is the balancing of actions. What we express into the world will come back to us to be experienced. In general, it's like being the recipient of our own actions. If we want to be loved and respected, well, we need to be loving and respectful. It's not all "instant karma" either. It could take time for karma to come home to us, and this is a gift. We are given time to reflect upon our life and make changes. This can interrupt the cycle of karma unless our soul decides the lesson is too valuable to miss. Karma can also be balanced through service. Meditating on this can give us insight on what our soul desires to accomplish and how it plans to do this. There is also a state of good karma. It is called dharma, and we reap its rewards just as automatically as we reap the lessons of karma.

Another side of forgiveness is more practical. The less we let go of our pain, and the harder we fight forgiving, the worse we will continue to feel. We punish ourselves when we punish another by holding a grudge.

Holding a grudge is a perfect description of the way being unforgiving acts on our physicality. The hurt, anger, and memory of betrayal are held in our body, locked in by our own tight grip. As we continue to live with the pain, it grows in us and molds our thoughts and beliefs to justify its presence with promises to protect us from any future insult or injury from that person. Eventually, it will begin to protect us from other people by creating feelings of fear and suspicion of them. We begin to lose our ability to see people as they are. They begin to look like the person who hurt us in the beginning. Our behavior will begin to change to support this pain we hold inside of us. We pick fights, cower from interactions, or withdraw

from opportunities to learn to trust again.

Whoa! Slipping into darkness is not letting our light shine. We go there anyway, don't we. Go ahead, get dark and sulk over your hurt, but promise yourself you will return and allow the hurt to heal. Believe in the light at the end of the tunnel, and it will be there for you when you are ready to see it.

> **"The less we let go of our pain and the harder we fight forgiving, the worse we will continue to feel."**

All in all, it's our emotions and beliefs about ourselves and the world that become our measuring stick for self-worth and worthiness. These judgements influence us as we position ourselves in relation to our fellow man and all the places we'd like to be. Like in the Glorious Child of God Club, for example.

Letting our light shine is about knowing who we are and standing solid in that knowing. One way to demonstrate that is to get acquainted with discernment. To know the difference between what is good for us and what isn't opens the path to trusting our own instincts and ability to make healthy decisions.

Here we can learn from the goddess Olivia. She is the Goddess of Evolution and has a message for us. She will teach us the power of learning how we create our outer lives from our inner thoughts and feelings. She wants us to gain control of the course of our lives by releasing the worries that burden us and negatively impact the materials we construct our reality with.

As you read her message, be open to the possibility that we are all changing in ways that will unlock our potential. It's an invitation to move past what we have learned to be true and real and to make room for different perspectives on life, creation, and our relationship to all that surrounds us. In her determination to set us free, she embodied the aspects of self-assuredness, compassion, preservation, and loyalty to growth. Olivia's message to us is one of adaptation for the purpose of allowing more love to flow in and out of us. There is no place for blindly repeating destructive patterns on the path to our future.

Olivia values her connection with Mother Earth and feels it in every strand of her DNA. She understands that Mother Earth represents our eternal mother who supports and nurtures us unconditionally and without judgement, and that she exists in part so we can live as a physical being for learning and evolving. We can connect with Mother Earth in the same way to renew this primal bond. Every time we ground and send our roots into the Earth, we allow our light to fill her, and we are showing her how much we love and appreciate her. This exchange helps the Earth renew herself and continue along her evolutionary path as well.

This month, we will explore the world of Aromatherapy as described by Jacki Smith. The science of Aromatherapy is fascinating and has a wonderful practical application in our lives. Jacki will share with us some first aid applications for the whole family. Using essential oils in our daily lives can bring harmony in the home and balance in our hearts and minds.

Mary & The Wood

by Jacki Smith

The glass rattling within the old wood
 . . . At each knock
I stand on your front doorstep
My baggage carefully wrapped
 For presentation.

I am the better soul,
 I have determined
For I have come with humility
Ready to lay down
 With the shame you expect
Created it to size, custom fit,
 (I've taken the measurements for years)

Patiently, I wait

Sizing up the door

With mental sketches of it's Renovation
Into the cross I plan to nail myself to
In penance for your grace

My script grasped
 within the hand of righteousness
I stand alert
Armed with well rehearsed words of
 self admonishment
Willing to accept your forgiveness
(As stated on page 14, line 20)

Smugly reviewing my position
All topics covered with
 Logic and explanations
Tailored to the response I desire

I am now ready to become the martyr.

July

Letting My Light Shine

Some Things To Do This Month

Be sensitive to the messages of your heart, they will help you to flow freely with life and make healthy decisions.

Build up your immune system now in preparation for the cold and flu season by eating foods in season. Try a Macrobiotic diet.

This is the month of rapid growth, so allow your emotions to develop and grow as well.

Living With Moon Energy

The Moon is the closest heavenly body to our planet. Her affect on us is real and immediate. Tracking the phases of the Moon and the zodiac sign she is traveling through can map out a cause and effect cycle for us. It will help make sense of our mood swings and patterns of luck, both good and bad.

Look up the Moon table on page 151 and record the date and zodiac sign the New and Full Moons are in.

Next, write down how you felt the three days around the New and Full Moons. Also record what was happening in your life at these times. Keeping track of this information will help you anticipate and prepare for future influences from the Moon. You may also compare your life with the interpretations provided on page 148.

**Notes on how the energy of the
New Moon and Full Moon affect me.**

July's Goddess

The evolutionary steps we have taken have been scrutinized to the best of our ability for a long time. We looked at our past and charted the physical, emotional, and mental progress of our existence in hopes that it will show us where we are going.

I believe what drives the grand evolution of all of humanity is the quiet evolution happening inside the body, mind, and heart of each individual, and this process happens before anything else changes in the world around us. If adaptability is the result of a subconscious response to what is not working, what are the possibilities when we move this response to our consciousness? It's a big question, and we will learn the answer together through exploration of our spirituality as well as the other factors that make up the reality we are experiencing. In meditation, you can begin the research of your own evolution. Ask Olivia to take you on a tour of your own adaptations and create a plan of change to insure a path of evolution in the direction that's right for you.

Meditation: For this meditation, you will need a dark green candle. Light the candle to serve as a beacon to call you back to the room when you have completed this journey. Close your eyes and begin to relax your muscles. With each breath, relax a different muscle group. Imagine yourself in a column of light that connects you to everything that reminds you of security and comfort. Next, imagine a new source of light emanating from the center of your body. It is your true essence and holds all of your experiences from the past, present, and future. It remains unchanged regardless of all the mutations your personality has gone through as a result of living. Allow this light to expand and merge with the column of light that surrounds you. You are now connected to the universe and have brought it home to your sacred space.

In this space you will find Olivia, the Goddess of Evolution. Call to her and ask her to connect with you for awhile. Once you feel her presence, ask her to show you one negative choice you have made or belief that has deviated you from your true path of evolution. Let it play out in your mind, and do your best to understand why you have made this choice. Then, ask Olivia to show you what you need to do to release you from this pattern and redirect your energy back to your original essence. Ask Olivia to give you any additional healing needed and update your energy with the changes you have just made. Ask that this healing begin with your separation from oneness, through all your experiences and back to your return to oneness.

When you feel complete with this experience, thank Olivia for her gift and release her back to the universe. Return from the meditation by slowly bringing your attention back to your body and to the room. Open your eyes and let the light of the candle bring you to full awareness. When you are ready, write about your experience on the July journal pages.

Olivia *Goddess of Evolution*

Evolution is a fact of life. Your genetic code and your connection to the Earth both played a necessary role in your survival. Both worked together behind the scenes to guide your development. Until now, it has been an unconscious adventure of cause and effect, driven by a force that seems beyond your control or even influence.

Things are changing for you now. For most of you, survival is not an issue. New frontiers are calling you now. The creative urge is awakening, and it is broad and expansive.

You are burgeoning on the horizon of a fantastic experience. You are becoming a creator in a whole new way. You are moving to a reality of consciously manifesting with your mind and emotions, and you must be prepared.

You will have to let go of many beliefs about yourself, your relationships with others, and of structure. You must be willing to be aware of what is truth and what has been created from illusion caused by fear. To get there, you will take many transformative steps. I will guide you. My name is Olivia, and I am the Goddess of Evolution.

"Your evolution is about adapting to the changing you. Let me liberate you from the outdated patterns that keep you from your destiny."

J U L Y

No matter what I choose, it is the right choice. The difference between choices is the direction they take me.

Letting my light shine

Family is our first experience of love. We have all come together with interchangeable roles of "Teacher" and "Student" to experience giving and receiving the very love that heals and binds all of us together.

J U L Y

I look through my past lives, the heritage of my ancestors, and the roots of my soul to find my highest self waiting there.

Aromatherapy

by Jacki Smith

What are you doing with your bottle of Lavender?

Through mistaken newscasters and overuse by mass marketed products, the term aromatherapy has been distilled down to refer to pleasant smells and mood enhancers. Although accurate, the use of essential oils in a therapy setting can go much deeper, into a healing level.

Many of us stand before the essential oil display in our local health food store, even purchasing our favorite

---

"Essential oils used for aromatherapy purposes can easily be incorporated into everyday living to help create well-being and a healthful balance"

---

scent, but still feeling daunted in the use of the oils for their therapeutic purposes. Essential oils used for aromatherapy purposes can easily be incorporated into everyday living to help create well-being and a healthful personal balance.

The first step to a balanced and healthful self is to unwind from the challenge of daily living. One way to achieve a calm and stress-free state is to put a few drops of Cypress, Marjoram, and Lavender in your bath. This is an oil combination that is best absorbed topically, so a bath is the optimal way to enhance their properties.

Sleep is another crucial element in your well-being. A few drops of Roman Chamomile on your pillow or nightclothes will help you fall asleep faster and deeper. This essential oil is also excellent for a sleep deprived mother and a cranky baby. One drop of Roman Chamomile on the collar of a baby's nightshirt can help your lullaby work faster. Another handy method is to squeeze out the oil from a vitamin E tablet into the palm of your hand and combine it with one drop of Lavender and one drop of Roman Chamomile. Gently massage the soles of the baby's feet, and watch calm restored to the household.

Put a few drops of Sandalwood in your shampoo to give yourself a spiritual lift in the morning or to decompress after a hectic day. Those same drops of oil could also be gently massaged into the scalp and combed through the hair to anoint and balance your crown chakra, pulling all the other chakras into alignment. An additional benefit is that Sandalwood will strengthen your hair while bringing spiritual enlightenment. For thinning hair, Rosemary oil rubbed on the scalp can promote hair growth and deter the rest from falling out!

Confidence can do wonders for a body. When you act with confidence, you are experiencing the positive influence of your personal power. In this state, emotional, spiritual, and physical healing take place. If a boost of confidence is needed, such as a job interview or any instance of needing to assert yourself, a blend of Jasmine, Orange, and Rose can help. Mix them together equally and place a drop on each wrist and behind the ear, and you become very attractive to others. This mixture will draw people to you and help you move forward to make the transition you desire.

If all the de-stressing, calming, uplifting, and confidence building don't block that cold that's going around, Lavender, Peppermint, Eucalyptus, Tee Tree, Frankincense, and Myrrh all work wonders against bacteria and viruses. They also ease the symptoms of a nasty cold. Get out your Vitamin E capsules and squeeze out the perfect amount of oil, mix in a few drops of any individual or combination of the above essential oils ,and gently rub it on your upper chest or right under your nose. Don't forget to make a mixture of Lemon, Eucalyptus, and water in a spray bottle to continually disinfect the open surfaces, phones, or any area that has come in contact with a sick person.

Even the healthiest person around will need first aid now and again. Bumps, bruises, minor cuts, and muscle aches are a part of living. Combine German Chamomile, Marjoram, and Eucalyptus with a squeeze of Vitamin E, and rub directly

onto the sore muscle, or drop in a bath for a good warm soak. Lavender is almost miraculous in the way it speeds healing, so place a few drops directly on a minor burn, scrape, or cut, and be amazed at how fast you heal. Enhance the speed of a bruise

---

"Lavender, Peppermint, Eucalyptus, Tee Tree, Frankincense, and Myrrh all work wonders against bacteria and viruses."

---

healing by combining Yarrow, Lavender, and the oil from a Vitamin E capsule and rubbing it directly onto the affected area.

Essential oils have so many valuable uses you may find yourself turning to them in your daily chores. Lavender and Peppermint sprinkled into your wash or onto a dryer sheet can eliminate tough odors, even that mildew smell. A blend of Sage, Coriander, and baking soda sprinkled onto your feet or in your shoes can even eliminate embarrassing foot odor. There is so much value in essential oils that a book or two on the subject can greatly expand your repertoire of healing uses.

You never want to replace the attention and advice of a good doctor with home remedies, so always consult your physician and seek emergency medical help when needed.

Jacki Smith is the founder of Coventry Creations, Inc. Jacki has been making aromatherapy candles in Michigan for over fifteen years. She also teaches self empowerment through the use of her products. You may reach her at:

www.coventrycreations.com.

Watching the Fruit of My Labor Ripen

Patience. Ask a woman late into her ninth month about patience. Waiting and shifting and waiting and sighing. Have another cup of tea? Did you try walking the floor . . . a lot?

Watching the fruit of my labor ripen may be the most anxious phase of creation for me. All the planning is done. All the pieces are put together. There is nothing left to do but wait, watch, and be ready for the birth or coming out.

"Waiting is an important part of creation. It is the time of magic."

That's where all the action is, but I'm not there yet, I'm here. Watching carefully, keeping myself busy, going over everything I already went over a dozen times. If I found a glitch, would I change it? Maybe, maybe not. At times like these, I will call in extra help with discipline so I don't fuss myself out of a masterpiece. Remember what happened to the soufflé? Too many peeks in the oven to see how it's doing was it's undoing. Poof! Flat as a pancake and a very disappointed chef.

Waiting is an important part of creation. It is the time of magic. This is when my creation takes on life and translates from idea into something

very real and tangible. I will be able to touch it, smell it, and take it in as a new experience. It will echo my ideas and imaginings, but until it is here, I will not know it. The anticipation of the outcome is exciting. Much like when I was pregnant, wondering what my child will look like. The physical manifestations of my ideas will be different than what my mind conceives, and that's the part that is magical to me. It makes the waiting worth it. I will be both surprised and pleased when I lay my eyes on the final outcome.

So many things are put into place during this waiting period. There is a ripening or maturing happening. As I resign myself to the space of watching, a sense of relief will come over me, and I'll welcome it. It's out of my hands now. I've done all I can, and like a new parent, I wait to see the results of all my work come back to me.

When this book went to the printer, I did not call them up screaming, "stop the presses" because I couldn't be calm and patient and let the book take form. Instead, I got out of the way and breathed. I breathed through my worries, my doubts, and my fears. And I prayed. I prayed for myself, the editor, the graphics team, the printer, the delivery person, everyone connected with this project. Finally, I let it go. How could it grow with me hovering over it, constantly changing it, and fussing over it?

"Finally, I affirm that I trust in a higher power and acknowledge that it will be there for me in a way beyond my greatest expectations."

A ritual that helped me focus my intention and create support while putting this project to bed was a candlelight vigil. I asked that the flame of the candle represent the love, joy, and protection available for my project. I lit it for a few hours a day until the project was complete. Then I surrendered the outcome along with any fear or anxiety to God and put the completed project into his loving hands and let it go.

Finally, I affirmed that I trust in a higher power and acknowledge that it will be there for me in ways beyond my greatest expectations. So, I let the mystery of creation do its thing while I waited, patiently holding the space of love and acceptance for my project.

A good and wise leader understands the importance of waiting. Honing our leadership skills for this phase of creation will support a desirable outcome. Amanda, the Goddess of Stewardship, embodies these qualities and teaches us about responsibility, creativity, and self-respect. Her message teaches us to align ourselves mentally and emotionally to become the leaders we are capable of being and realize our part in the plan. Partake in her meditation for guidance when faced with a challenge

or when you need help attaining your goal.

This month the featured article is about what herbs and vitamins are safe to use during pregnancy. I am pleased to present Jann Sumner. Jann is an Herbalist and Certified Doula (Professional Labor and Birth Support) and shares with us her knowledge. Even if you are not expecting at this time, the information is very interesting and something you can save for later or pass along to other women.

A Lone Woman
by Jacki Smith

Good morning
  to the quiet house,
  the slow pace,

Alone with my thoughts
Alone with my dreams

Good morning
  to myself

Tea in hand
  I reach for the day
Alone
  quiet
    on my own

A
  Lone
    Woman
riding on strength,
supported by doubt
so quiet
no voices

Soon
  I shall have to
    remember
      how to speak

Watching the Fruit of My Labor Ripen

Some Things To Do This Month

Learn the depth of your power and become a courageous leader in your own right.

The raspberries are ripe and ready for harvest. Drink raspberry leaf tea to help reduce female problems and balance your blood sugar.

Our tendency is to multi-task ourselves into a frenzy. Prioritize and trust your natural cycle for rest and work.

Living With Moon Energy

The Moon is the closest heavenly body to our planet. Her affect on us is real and immediate. Tracking the phases of the Moon and the zodiac sign she is traveling through can map out a cause and effect cycle for us. It will help make sense of our mood swings and patterns of luck, both good and bad.

Look up the Moon table on page 151 and record the date and zodiac sign the New and Full Moons are in.

Next, write down how you felt the three days around the New and Full Moons. Also record what was happening in your life at these times. Keeping track of this information will help you anticipate and prepare for future influences from the Moon. You may also compare your life with the interpretations provided on page 148.

Notes on how the energy of the New Moon and Full Moon affect me.

August's Goddess

Leadership is not just about achieving the goal, it's also about how we got there. Malfunctioning group dynamics are just as detrimental to success as conflicting outside influences. A leader, who sees herself as a steward, recognizes the importance of this and knows that the individuals in the group are working with her and not just for her. A steward is sensitive to the many levels of leadership required and has her thumb on the pulse on each one of them. She also knows the wisdom in seeking advice from her team, her peers, and her mentors. In the following meditation, you will have the opportunity to meet with someone who has harnessed the meaning of stewardship. She teaches us to incorporate love and compassion in our leadership styles and shows that if we pull from the strengths of the group, we are more successful and satisfied. Meet with Amanda, and let her show you the rewards of stewardship.

Meditation: For this meditation, put a gold candle on a table near you and light it. It represents the depth and wisdom of stewardship. To prepare to meet Amanda, sit in a straight-backed chair with your feet flat on the floor and begin breathing deeply and slowly. Soon you will notice where your body is tense. Relax each tense muscle by contracting and releasing it, and allow your body to feel more fluid and heavy. After your body feels relaxed, release all the chatter from your mind. Observe your thoughts as they float away. When you notice that you are free of random thoughts, know that you have relaxed your mind and are ready to receive Amanda's messages.

Now, bring your attention to the center of your body. Notice a bright ball of light illuminating your stomach and heart. Imaging that light growing larger and filling your entire body. Next, imagine it growing larger and filling the space around you. Let it expand until you feel it is large enough to provide you with a safe space to work in. Now, call upon your spirit guides to surround and protect you. Return your breathing to your normal rhythm and visualize yourself sitting in a beam of light that originates from above you and goes far below your feet. Next, visualize an identical beam of light three feet in front of you. Within that beam you begin to see a face and then the body of a strong and kind woman. She smiles and begins sending you feelings of friendship and acceptance. This is Amanda. When you are ready, send a thin stream of light from your heart to hers. Let this heart connection bring to your consciousness all she is here to share with you. Accept Amanda's message knowing that it may reveal itself more fully over time. The gold candle will act as a trigger to your memory each time you light it. When you are ready to end the meditation, release Amanda with your thanks, and slowly return your attention to your body and then the room. Stretch and breathe a deep cleansing breath. Record your impressions on the journal pages while they are still fresh in your mind.

Amanda *Goddess of Stewardship*

There comes a time in your life when you must take the lead, even if it's just for a moment. Some of you may jump at the chance to be in charge while others cringe at the thought. Even the most enthusiastic leaders meet their wall of resistance. That is when I can be of service to you. I am the Goddess of Stewardship, and I am here to teach the art of leading.

Leadership is an opportunity to direct a situation and work toward a specific outcome. It is also an opportunity to learn about people, especially yourself.

In the role of leader, you are caregiver, decision-maker, and delegator. Inspiration and responsibility rests on your shoulders.

If you take the attitude that you are the steward of the situation, you will find it easier to bring all involved into a cooperative effort. As steward, you are acting in service just as much as you are in authority. This means that you never lose sight of the importance of your team while holding the vision of the goal.

The role of leader is a powerful place to be. Acting as a steward means being there in service as well as control.

Because we come from a place of innocence about how life works, we set ourselves upon a lifelong quest to learn what it is to live joyfully.

Watching the fruit of my labor ripen

*Gentle kisses of the angel caress the spirit
and enlighten the soul.*

A U G U S T

I forgive all events that have disappointed me and have learned their lessons.

Watching the fruit of my labor ripen

*Understanding the rhythm of nature is the basis
for all wisdom.*

PREGNANCY, NUTRITION, AND HERBS: WHAT'S SAFE?

By Jan Sumner, Herbalist & Doula
(member of Doulas of North America)

As an Herbalist and a Doula (professional Labor and Birth Support), I get asked about herbal remedies and which are safe to use for minor complaints during pregnancy. Although many herbs are generally quite safe for the non-pregnant body, special considerations must be accounted for when a woman is housing a baby. Like medications, herbs can cross the placenta and enter into the baby's system, and care must be taken when weighing out the need to treat either conventionally or naturally.

> **"Although many herbs are generally quite safe, special considerations must be accounted for when a woman is housing a baby."**

The following are supplements that I feel are necessary and safe when pregnant and what I recommend to my clients. A pregnant woman needs approximately 2300 calories per day, and no matter whether she is a vegetarian or not, these calories should come from a variety of nutritional sources. If a woman is a vegetarian, extra B12 should be taken. Her diet should be high in calcium and iron and contain at least 75 grams of protein per day from either plant or meat sources. Protein is essential for brain development in the baby, and particular care should be taken by the mother each day to ensure that she is eating enough to support this. Calcium is important not only for the development of the baby's bones and teeth, but it also helps to ensure a healthy heart in the mother, who's heart size increases by 20% while pregnant to accommodate the extra blood volume. Magnesium is very important as well as a preventative of pre-eclampsia and preterm labor, and a dose of 300 mgs per day should be included in the diet. 800 mcg of Folic acid per day is very important as well to prevent low birth weight babies and babies with neural tube defects such as spina bifida.

I recommend that women take a good organic source of iron while pregnant to prevent anemia but no more than 30 mgs per day is required unless your caregiver tells you otherwise. A good multi-vitamin designed for pregnancy is a good idea as well, but you should adjust the above mentioned supplements if they are included in it as it is important not to take more than needed.

There are times while pregnant that situations arise that may need some treatments. I usually recommend that a woman speak to her midwife or doctor before taking anything for a serious matter, but there are some herbs which can be safely used for minor complaints, preventatives, and for labor. Here is a short list of complaints and some remedies, which are safe and effective, when taken as directed on the bottle or as indicated.

High Blood Pressure: If you are starting to experience Pregnancy Induced High Blood Pressure (PIH), and your caregiver says that it's OK for you to try a natural supplement to lower it, try either garlic in capsule form with a high allicin content or evening primrose oil. Evening primrose oil should only be used in the last month, however, as it does

---

"The best thing for nausea or vomiting, pregnant or not, is ginger. Vitamin B6 also helps to prevent morning sickness."

---

ripen the cervix and can bring on early labor in very rare cases.

Nausea: The best thing for nausea or vomiting, pregnant or not, is ginger. Studies have shown that even hyperemensis gravidarum, which is the most severe form of pregnancy related nausea and vomiting, was reduced significantly in 19 out of 27 pregnant women when taken 4 times per day. It can be made into a tea by chopping up a one-inch piece of the root, pouring about 3 cups of boiling water over it, and steeping for 20 minutes. The tea can be mixed with some lemon and honey to taste. If you find this tea a bit strong, you can purchase ginger capsules or tablets and take it that way as well. Vitamin B6 also helps to prevent morning sickness, and up to 200 mgs per day

can safely be taken up to the time of birth, when the dose should be cut down to 50 mgs per day as high doses of B6 can interfere with lactation.

Colds or Flus: Echinacea is safe when used for short periods of time while pregnant and may be used at the first sign of a virus to lessen its duration and severity. Always use a tincture form and take as directed for no more than one week. Garlic is a very good antiviral and may also be taken for the duration of the virus safely while pregnant.

Depression, Anxiety, etc: Vitamin B6 is nature's Prozac and is safe to take while pregnant. A dose of up to 200 mgs per day can be taken to combat depression or anxiety, but this dose should be cut back to 50 mgs per day at time of the birth as high doses of B6 can interfere with lactation. Vitamin B6 is very beneficial for postpartum depression as well. A B complex vitamin high in B6 would be an excellent idea!

Leg Cramps and Varicose Veins: Nettle is very beneficial for treating varicose veins by strengthening blood vessels. It is also very high in vitamins and minerals, including calcium and iron. It can be used throughout pregnancy for energy, alleviating leg cramps, preventing

---

"Vitamin B6 is very beneficial for postpartum depression. "

---

anemia, and decreasing the chance of hemorrhage during childbirth.

Labor preparation: Red raspberry leaf is fabulous for toning the uterus and aiding with breast-feeding. It is rich in vitamins, minerals, and high in chelated iron. It tones the uterus, increases the flow of milk, and helps to restore a woman's reproductive system after childbirth. It is the number one recommended herbal tonic for pregnancy and breast-feeding! It can be made into a tea and drank freely throughout pregnancy and labor. It is also beneficial with the prevention of miscarriage.

Evening primrose oil, because of its effects on the body's prostaglandin production, helps to soften the cervix (efface) in preparation for dilation and birth. Taken in the last month of pregnancy, it can be very effective for this purpose. You can safely take 8 capsules per day in the last month.

Prevention of miscarriage: While not all miscarriages can be prevented, and many first trimester miscarriages are due to malformed embryos, there are times when a woman's body simply won't carry a pregnancy due to things like lack of uterine tone, rejection of the implantation, etc., and there are some herbs that she can take to try to prevent miscarriage. False unicorn tones the uterus before, during, and after the pregnancy and is very safe to take for prevention of miscarriage. It is also very good at boosting fertility and should not be given to women where pregnancy wouldn't be advisable. It will also increase sperm production. Red raspberry is also very good for prevention of miscarriage and can be taken freely throughout early, mid, and late pregnancy. A doctor should always investigate habitual miscarriage (more than 3).

While there are safe herbs for pregnancy, there are also many that are not safe, and some that are quite dangerous. They are too vast to

mention them all, so I will supply a short list of common herbs that are contraindicated during pregnancy. There are always exceptions to this rule of course, and a licensed naturopath trained in childbirth or a midwife may prescribe some of these herbs safely under close supervision, but these herbs should never be used while self-treating.

They are: Black Cohosh, Blue Cohosh, Cascara, Dong Quai, Ephedra, Feverfew, Ginseng, Goldenseal, Licorice, Lobelia, Senna, or Yarrow. If you are uncertain that what you want

---

"Pregnancy is a wonderful journey that brings the life of a baby into the world. It is not a illness, it is a naturally occurring condition."

---

to take is safe, always ask an experienced midwife, herbalist, or naturopath trained in pregnancy and childbirth, and if all else fails, and you can't find the answers, don't take the herb.

Pregnancy and childbirth is a wonderful journey that brings the life of a baby into the world. It is not a illness, it is a naturally occurring condition that should be coveted by all that walk its path. In addition to practicing healthy eating, taking supplements, and moderate exercise, it is important to surround yourself with good prenatal care, education about what is happening and going to happen, and loving support during labor and birth. Your partner and a trained doula can do much to ensure an optimum outcome and a joyous event, to be remembered by you as one of the best experiences in your life.

What is at the Root of It All?

When you suspect root rot, it's best to take a peek under the turf. After a few years of single parenting, a new career, and dating, I was exhausted and succumbing to the effects of too much stress. My symptoms were non-specific, and parts weren't falling off, but I just couldn't keep up with my life anymore. When my stomach went on strike, I chose to see a Naturopath. The first consultation was heavenly. We spent a few hours just talking about me. That alone did me a world of good.

"My body was so confused from the stress, poor eating habits, and lack of regeneration time, that it forgot how to heal itself and needed retraining."

But, I needed more. My body was so confused from the stress, poor eating habits, and lack of regeneration time that it forgot how to heal itself and needed retraining. Upon her guidance and recommendations, I went home with a bag of homeopathic remedies, Bach Flower tinctures, a list of teas and herbs to purchase at the health food store, and suggestions for a new lifestyle.

The new lifestyle was on special at my local health food store, but they didn't have my size so I had to custom design one for myself. I had to make time for the essentials I had been putting off for some obscure future. First of all, I had to stop worrying so much.

Second, I had to exercise. The curative forces of exercise surprised me. My Naturopath told me that my body used movement to complete its chemical processes. It aids in digestion and absorption of nutrients. It even helps keep my bones strong. I should have paid attention in health class. Needless to say, it worked. Nothing like results to seal the deal.

Third, I had to eat my fruits and vegetables. An acquired taste, but I'm getting them down. Now I won't have to be the hypocrite at the dinner table anymore.

These lifestyle changes are common sense, and I could get this information from a cereal box, but what made the difference for me was doing it. Making the changes even when I was too tired or depressed was the key to my success. It boiled down to taking care of myself and making a commitment to living, not just functioning. Anyway, it took illness and the firm guidance of a caring friend to get me to pay attention.

Yes, the Naturopath saved my life, though she would blush to hear me say that. She was just grateful I showed up when I did. To make sure I was completely grounded in the seriousness of my condition, she quietly told me I had just avoided a trip to the hospital. I continued to heal under her care and returned to the level of health I enjoyed pre-crash.

"I didn't intend for it to be dramatic. I was going to start out with some chamomile tea for stress or maybe take garlic during the flu season."

That was my introduction to alternative therapies. I didn't intend for it to be dramatic. I was going to start out with some chamomile tea for stress or maybe take garlic during the flu season, but I waited too long and whammo, root rot.

It's wise to check the condition of your roots periodically. They tell you a lot about yourself and can help prevent a health crisis. Some very revealing questions to ask yourself are: How am I feeling? Do I feel rested after eight hours sleep? Can I digest my food without pain? How many headaches do I get a week? Am I happy? Keep yourself healthy with exercise, a balanced diet, and a happy disposition. Above all, when you don't feel well, ask for help.

Sarah, our Goddess of Sisterhood, invites you to join her in a meditation honoring the divine connection between women. You are part of a great gathering of women who value and support each other. Sarah asks you to reach out to them and find your ability to be a true sister through compassion. She also yearns for you to let your sisters take care of you and break down the walls that hold out the happiness. This can be accomplished by letting someone love you. Start with the sisterhood and grow from there.

This month we will explore the benefits of Homeopathic Medicine. Of all the alternative therapies I have explored, I have the most experience with homeopathy. It was instrumental in bringing my body into balance, strengthening my immune system, and working to correct genetic patterns passed down the family tree that were blocking my healthy picture.

I sing the praises of homeopathy because it has made such a dramatic difference for me. I have had the privilege of working with a very talented and intuitive doctor of Homeopathy, Laura Lohman Gannan. In Laura's article, she gives excellent practical suggestions for treating many typical health issues that challenge us and our families daily. Try some of her recommendations and feel the difference.

Monuments to the Day
by Jacki Smith

I can see the sparkles
  as they flit
    in & out of my body

I can feel the tingling
  over my skin

I can see excitement
  building monuments
    to the day

A good day

September

What is at the root of it all?

Some Things To Do This Month

Use good judgement, discernment, and fairness when reasoning out decisions.

Try violet leaf tea for sore throats, stomach-aches, or bowel problems. This great little plant is also beneficial for the skin.

Protect yourself with the good sense that like attracts like. Undo negative situations with unconditional love.

Living With Moon Energy

The Moon is the closest heavenly body to our planet. Her affect on us is real and immediate. Tracking the phases of the Moon and the zodiac sign she is traveling through can map out a cause and effect cycle for us. It will help make sense of our mood swings and patterns of luck, both good and bad.

Look up the Moon table on page 151 and record the date and zodiac sign the New and Full Moons are in.

Next, write down how you felt the three days around the New and Full Moons. Also record what was happening in your life at these times. Keeping track of this information will help you anticipate and prepare for future influences from the Moon. You may also compare your life with the interpretations provided on page 148.

**Notes on how the energy of the
New Moon and Full Moon affect me.**

September's Goddess

Women are in the midst of a struggle. We want it all: family, career, freedom, commitment, security, love, health, stamina, support, happiness, and four weeks vacation a year. How is this possible? The sisterhood. Women helping women. Be the sister you have always wanted and needed, and then open up and ask for help. It's quite a different experience than trying to do it all on your own.

Eligibility for this club takes a promise though. You have to promise to stop the demeaning competition and sabotage, and tame the jealousy monster. Yes, there is need for some healing here. Learning to trust another woman will mean letting go of the past. Mother may have hurt you, but you do not have to stay hurt. Let yourself heal. Allow another woman to help you with this. It can be your first step to acknowledging that the possibility of a sisterhood is real.

No matter what your experiences with other women have been, in the sisterhood there is only compassion for each other. Seek out Sarah in this meditation. Ask her about this dynamic network of women, and she can help you heal the wounds that keep you disconnected from your sisters.

Meditation: You will need a white candle and a mirror. Light the candle and begin your slow, deep breathing to relax. Let go of your stress with each exhale. Upon each inhale, envision a white light coming up from below your feet and down from above your head. Imagine the white light filling you, then expanding and filling the room. Return to normal breathing and bring your attention to the center of your body. Visualize a bright light shining there. Watch it grow and expand, filling your body and then filling the room. As it meets the light in the room, the two sources of light merge and become one. This is your sacred space, and you have complete control and authority of everything that happens here. If you desire, invite your guardian angel or another spiritual protector to be with you.

Now, imagine a bridge of pink light spanning from your heart to a lush garden encircled by a low stone wall. Standing in front of the gate is a woman, and you can see many women gathering in the distance behind her. She beckons you to join her. When you are ready, cross the bridge to the garden and greet this woman you've come to realize is Sarah.

Sarah leads you to a bench, and you both sit to talk. With large luminous eyes, she waits patiently for you to ask your question or ask for a healing. Listen carefully to her answers or open up to receive her healing. Once you feel complete, thank Sarah and take some time to visit with the other women in the garden. After your visit, walk back across the light bridge and allow it to dissolve. Bring your attention back to the room and look into the mirror. See Sarah's luminous eyes in your eyes and remember the advice she gave you. Record everything in the journal pages.

Sisterhood. A very old-fashioned concept indeed, and yet, it is still one that is very much needed. Belonging to the sisterhood means having a special connection with other women. It is a commitment that goes deep, as deep as the secrets you keep for each other. It is validation as you explore the many experiences being a woman will bring to you.

My name is Sarah, and I am the Goddess of Sisterhood. I have come to initiate you into a collective of women that spreads far and wide and knows no ethnic, cultural, or religious boundaries.

Come, learn to be with women who know how to nurture. Let their love heal you in a way that reaches to your soul and paves the way to the Mother God.

I am here. Allow me to prepare you for the true and sustaining love you have longed for. I will do this by helping you heal the hurts caused by the misconceptions of motherhood, sisterhood, and being a woman.

Come join me in the healing, nurturing womb of the sisterhood. We will band together to heal ourselves and then the world.

SEPTEMBER

Good Karma takes effort and commitment to personal healing.

What is at the root of it all?

All possibilities exist within the dream dimensions.
A better way awaits your light.

S E P T E M B E R

*A crisp autumn night begins with a sunset that dazzles your senses
and heightens your awareness of the world around you.*

What is Homeopathy?

By Laura Lohman-Gannan, RSHom(NA), CCH

Homeopathy is a form of medicine that uses natural substances from plants, animals, or minerals to create remedies. Each remedy is prepared by a specific dilution method whose action gently stimulates the body to heal itself. Homeopaths believe that the body can heal itself of disease when the remedy that matches the symptoms is given. This is referred to as like curing like. If you have a cold with runny eyes and nose, we might select Allium Cepa, which is the red onion. When you cut an onion, what happens? The idea being that what can cause symptoms in a healthy person can cure a sick person with the same symptoms. This concept is both simple and complex, and the more you learn of homeopathy, the more you learn how broad its application is from curing the simplest cold to other more serious conditions.

Most importantly, YOU can try this at home!

The idea behind this almanac is to provide people with useful resources for healing their lives. Homeopathy is one with a no-side-effect approach for everyday health challenges.

What Do You Do?

I believe most of us would like to live healthy lives and do what is right for our bodies. We are bombarded with information about toxins and the overuse of antibiotics, radiation, pesticides, drugs, and candida. We walk through health food stores, and we are hit with a barrage of products and techniques. You often wonder where to start and what to do to help yourself achieve good health. I offer homeopathy as an approach that will make you feel brave and confident enough to begin to take charge of your health one step at a time.

Homeopathy is vast, and trying to understand it completely takes some time, but I invite you to begin to treat simple challenges like bumps and bruises, aches and pains, earaches, sore throats, sinus pain, etc. Give these suggestions a try, and with each success, you will build confidence that you can help your body heal itself. Then you can consider taking classes or buying books, and begin to enter this wonderful world of healing naturally.

Homeopathy is over 200 years old, and the same remedies you are using were used then. You have a huge database of results from around the world of remedies for these illnesses.

Flu and Colds: Protect yourself during flu season with *Influenzinum* 200c 1 time a week. If not available, try *Arsenicum Iodatum*. At the first sign of any virus, repeat the remedy every hour. If symptoms decrease after three doses, repeat only as necessary. In homeopathy, you reduce or discontinue a remedy when symptoms reduce or go away.

Bumps and Bruises: Your two-year-old just fell and has a goose egg on his/her forehead. Give *Arnica Montana* 30-200c immediately and up to three doses the day of injury. In the morning, you may find no sign of injury or just a small bruise! Continue remedy for one more day. *Arnica* helps prevent head trauma in addition to preventing blood pooling in the tissues which creates inflammation and bruising. Great for your athletic children and other family members. Use 30c potency before or after a game with lots of contact to prevent chronic injury patterns. *Arnica* cream may be used on sport injuries as well.

Bee Stings: Sudden swelling accompanied by heat to the area. Give *Apis* 30c and you should see swelling decline in 30 minutes. *Ledum* is good if *Apis* fails.

Pulled Tendons: Too much running, tennis, walking? Try *Ruta Graviolis* 30c-200c three times a day for a week. If you have a chronic injury, it may take longer, or there may be other things to consider. It also can be effective for wrist fatigue from overuse with the computer or typewriter.

Ear Aches: It's two in the morning, and your baby is screaming, her head is hot with fever, and her ear is fiery red. *Belladonna* 30c can calm things down in one hour. You may need to repeat the dose. Or your baby is crying, and nothing will satisfy him/her. One cheek is hot, and the other is cold. *Chamomile* should do the trick and

repeat the dose if necessary. Or if your baby has drainage out of her ear and wants to be carried and comforted, use *Pulsatilla*. Triumphs in the middle of the night with homeopathic remedies have made true believers of many parents!

Vomiting: You are on vacation, and everyone gets sick. *Ipecac* 30c repeated every hour for three hours can often save the day or night! Good for vomiting during pregnancy too!

"I invite you to begin to treat simple challenges like bumps and bruises, aches and pains, earaches, sore throats, and sinus pain"

Diarrhea: *Podophyllum* 30c works like a charm. Also a prophylactic for liver cancer. If you have "oops!" and "poops", try *Veratrum Album* 30c.

Seasickness: Afraid to travel by boat? *Cocculus* has given relief to many. Try 12c or 30c repeated throughout the day. I have heard some wonderful testimonials for this remedy.

Fear and Anxiety: For our moments of anxiety, try *Aconite*. Many cases of panic disorder have been resolved with *Aconite* 6c, 12, 30c, or 200c. If you have suffered a fright or have asthma with anxiety, this is worth considering.

Smelly Feet: Afraid to take off your shoes? Try *Silica* 30c three times a day for one to two weeks, and SMELL the difference. May need to be continued! Never suppress foot sweats with powders! This can lead to serious problems. Why would you push back what the body is trying to remove?

Performance Anxiety: Going to give a speech but you fear an attack of diarrhea or stage fright? *Gelsenium* is the ticket. Take at least one hour before the performance. What a lifesaver! Great for children too!

Allergies: *Arsenicum Iodatum* 30c daily. Especially good if you get a runny nose, skin reaction, or stomach sensitivity.

Food Poisoning: *Arsenicum* 30c repeated. Great for mystery foods on airplanes that "rumble" later.

Skin Rashes and Irritation: Scratching until it bleeds? Try *Sulfur* 30c twice a day for a week and watch for improvement.

PMS: Craving for salt or chocolate and experiencing symptoms such as anger or headaches? *Nat Mur* 30c repeated a few days before your period starts could be great!

Menopausal Hot Flashes: Burning up with sweat day and night? *Lachesis* 30c three times a day. Many women find it relieves symptoms and can eliminate the need for estrogen. Try it for one to two weeks for results.

Depression: Are you overworked? Do you find yourself yelling at your family a lot? *Sepia* 30c each day will make you feel like a human being again.

Grief and Loss: Any loss great or small can be helped with *Ignatia* 30x. Take it three times a day for one week to keep your healing process healthy.

You are now armed with powerful tools which will serve you well. Homeopathy will cure you gently and safely. If you have serious or chronic problems, consult with a good homeopath in your area. Many homeopaths are being certified and have the initials CCH after their name. You may contact the National Center for Homeopathy in Virginia for more information.

Remedies are available at most health food stores. You may order through Dolisos in Nevada by calling 1 800 DOLISOS.

This information is provided for educational purposes. If you have serious health problems, are pregnant, or using drugs, please consult with your physician.

Laura Lohman-Gannan, RSHom (NA) CCH lives, breathes and eats homeopathy. She has been privileged to study with exceptional homeopaths from the eastern and western worlds. She makes homeopathy simple and practical. Her vision for you is that your inner and outer health be in perfect harmony. Living in awareness is the ultimate experience for you and is the signature of her work.

For consultation information contact Laura at:
(248) 203-7123
e-mail: officecall @aol.com

Autumn

September 21st - December 20th

Season of Strength and Evaluation

As we enter the season of great beauty and transformation, take the time to look around you and watch how nature cares for itself and prepares for the coming winter. You will also start your own transition into the introspective months of winter, but you must prepare first. As momentum for growth is slowed, and energy is consolidated, you will focus inward for completion of thoughts and ideas.

Now is the time to evaluate the quality of what you've accomplished the past seven months and determine what needs to be done next. Feel the strength of your position in life. You have chosen a path or direction and now are fulfilling your commitment to it.

Burn sage leaves to purify your thoughts, emotions, and the space around you. This will help you "see" honestly the progress you have made this year.

Invite the Grizzly Bear totem animal into your meditations. Allow it to show you where your strengths and weaknesses are and the best way to continue successfully.

Suggestions for Optimal Seasonal Health

Physical   Treat seasonal allergies seriously with a trip to a homeopath or naturopath. Relief will be yours. Tai Chi or yoga will relieve muscle strain and increase your strength.

Emotional   The changing season can bring anxiety. Life takes on a different pace, and the demands can make you feel tense. Pamper yourself with your favorite relaxation technique. It could be a rousing game of basketball or a quiet soak in the tub. The choice is yours, but just do it!

Mental   The energy of the season pulls you inward for self-evaluation. If your mind is cluttered with a negative self-image, you will not be able to be objective. Throw out the old to make room for the new with positive affirmations of self-love.

Spiritual   Once you have removed your mask of who you thought you were, retreat inward on a spiritual journey and discover who you are. It will be filled with surprises and some things you need to forgive. Be gentle with yourself on the tough stuff and rejoice for the wonderful stuff.

Solving Mysteries

Many things in life are a mystery to me. That's why I read a lot. I ask a lot of questions, too. My children reminded me about questions. They asked me thousands of questions, daily. When they became teenagers, they reminded me about the art of asking questions. To get the answers you are looking for, you have to ask the right question to the right source. This takes good observation skills, clarity, courage, perseverance, and a real desire to know the truth.

Now solving mysteries can be a grand hobby that fills your head with fascinating facts, but it can also serve you well on your path to self-awareness. This leads us to your first question. Why do I want to be self-aware?

Self-awareness is the act of healing. It allows us to become aware of the level of love, hate, pain, fear, and dissociation we carry within our psyche. This is important to us because these captive emotions mold and twist the development of our body and mind. For example, a physical manifestation of hate can turn up in a wart, as cancer, or the desire for revenge. The way love manifests is in health, happiness, compassion, and courage.

The path of healing feels like we're solving mysteries because much of what hurts is hidden from your consciousness. We detach ourselves from painful experiences and submerge them into our subconscious in order to cope and survive. Later, when we are strong enough to heal from our issues, we have to follow the trail of clues to find the root cause or original experience. It is from that place that we complete the healing and make space for our true selves to live.

". . . a physical manifestation of hate can show up as a wart or as cancer or the desire for revenge."

This leads us to our next question. Why am I sick, poor, unhappy, unlucky, alone, etc? All of these conditions in our life are actually an outward expression of the deeply held beliefs we have about ourselves.

Over the course of our life, certain things happen to us that define who we are and our relationship with the world around us. If our parents were nurturing and supportive, we will grow up to be comfortable with and accepting of love and support from others. We will build our life from knowing that we belong and are cherished, and the outward condition of our life will reflect this.

Disappointments will be shouldered with a higher degree of confidence, and we will see our challenges and sufferings as life lessons or opportunities to improve ourselves.

"The answers to all our probing questions come from within . . . They are disguised as the pain locked in our body, emotions, and mind"

On the other hand, if we begin our lives with hardships, our will to attain our potential is thwarted, and we could begin to question our worth.

Our ancestors' beliefs and attitudes about themselves also mold us. If our parents were poor and depressed, we may decide that this is our fate as well. Looking for clues to help us define our issues can also be found in our beliefs about our parents, grandparents, and even siblings. They are the broader signals or signposts that tell us, "look here for more information about what makes up the you that you have become."

The answers to all our probing questions come from within, even the ones about our families and the greater world around us. They are there disguised as the pain locked in our body, layered in our emotions, and trapped in our mind. They come to us as metaphors, symbols, and memories. There is wisdom within us that can unravel the puzzles and lead us to understanding and resolution. Our answers are also accessed through conversations with our soul, spirit guides, and our creator.

Our goddess for October is Kristen. We call her the Goddess of Shadow and Light because she teaches that we are both dark and light. It is in our shadow that we safely store the pain of our past, and it is our light that brings healing to that past.

Kristen embodies the virtues of strength, courage, and ingenuity. Her meditation will bring us her blessings of protection and encouragement for each trial and test we endure. Connect with Kristen any time you need support in facing your fears while delving into your personal history.

After the journal pages, I have included an article about using crystals and stones as healing tools. I have worked with crystals in this capacity for over ten years, and I am still learning more about them. So, go have some fun with crystals and do a little healing too!

A Woman Alone

by Jacki Smith

The sound
of my voice
    jumps in my ears
vibrates through my
bones

It's been so
quiet here
Hushed
    to the silence
of a woman alone
Solitude
    to be claimed
    and empowered
Remembering how to

speak
how my lips
    and tongue
move in unison
responding to
    air
passing through
    my mouth
I utter one word . . . .

October

Solving Mysteries

Some Things To Do This Month

Look within and connect with the hurts that block your happiness. One way to set these parts free is to give them a voice and unconditional love.

Keep in touch with who you are and stay centered as you make important decisions

Feeling nervous with all this soul searching? Try some mullein tea to calm that jittery tummy.

Living With Moon Energy

The Moon is the closest heavenly body to our planet. Her affect on us is real and immediate. Tracking the phases of the Moon and the zodiac sign she is traveling through can map out a cause and effect cycle for us. It will help make sense of our mood swings and patterns of luck, both good and bad.

Look up the Moon table on page 151 and record the date and zodiac sign the New and Full Moons are in.

Next, write down how you felt the three days around the New and Full Moons. Also record what was happening in your life at these times. Keeping track of this information will help you anticipate and prepare for future influences from the Moon. You may also compare your life with the interpretations provided on page 148.

**Notes on how the energy of the
New Moon and Full Moon affect me.**

October's Goddess

We created our shadowselves out of our more painful experiences and hold them in our subconscious to keep them from interfering with our daily life. However, sometimes this is not the case. When something occurs in our life that resonates with the past, old feelings begin to stir, rise up, and then merge with the feelings we are having in the current situation. Eventually, we find our actions loaded with emotions that don't add up. When we heal our shadowselves, our lives begin to make more sense. During the following meditation, you will be challenged to look at some experiences you hoped would stay forgotten. Some of them will be relatively easy, while others will require professional counseling. Treat yourself with love and respect, and ask for help when it's time.

Meditation: You will need a river stone about the size of an egg and a blue candle. Place the stone between your feet. Sit with your feet flat on the floor and your back straight. This will help you stay in your body during this meditation. Light the blue candle for courage. Now, begin breathing deeply and slowly to release all tension from your body and extraneous thoughts from your mind.

Begin visualizing a bright ball of light illuminating the center of your body. Allow it to expand to fill and surround you with love and protection. Feel yourself becoming connected to the Earth and the source of love. Call upon your spirit guides for support during this meditation.

When you are ready, imagine you are sitting comfortably in your favorite place. All of your favorite things are there, and you feel safe. Off in the distance, you notice a woman. She smiles at you and waits for an invitation to enter your sacred space. When you feel ready, invite Kristen over and tell her you would like to heal your shadowself. She will point to a dark figure at the edge of your favorite place. With Kristen by your side, walk over to the figure and ask her to tell you her story. With compassion for this part of you, listen closely to her experience. Thank her for holding this memory for you. Her sacrifice allowed you to go on with your life. Next, ask her if she's ready to be freed from the experience, heal the related pain, and rejoin you. If the answer is yes, watch Kristen surround your shadowself with light and remove all her burdens. When you and this separate part of you are ready, merge with one another and come closer to wholeness. If the answer is no, respect this decision and ask Kristen to take this part of you to your higher self to hold. You can work with this issue another time.

Conclude this meditation with Kristen with gratitude for her help and release her out of your sacred space. Return your attention to your body and then the room. Stretch and take a cleansing breath. When your head clears record your thoughts and feelings on the journal pages.

Kristen
goddess of shadow & light

What is darkness, but just the absence of light. What is light, but the presence of love.

I understand why you become frightened in the dark and run from it. It holds all the things that have made you feel small and powerless. It reminds you of your pain and fear.

Navigating the dark corners of your psyche takes skill and courage. If you allow me, I will teach you how to face the darkness and show you how it can become a teacher, protector, and nurturer.

My name is Kristen, and I know the importance of the shadow as well as the light. In my manifestation, I bring the truth about your shadowself and your light. I will show you what you hide in the your deep, dark recesses and shine the light of your own living soul upon it. Not to frighten you, but to help you face it and heal.

This is the way to befriend the darkness. This is the way to be free of its negative hold and live your life the way you've known you are meant to live it.

Love is all there is, even in the dark.
I will shine light into your
shadowself and show you
the power of love.

O C T O B E R

Magic is not from an external source, but from deep within.

Solving mysteries

Listen to the song in your heart, it sings the truth.

O C T O B E R

My heart's rhythm guides me, imparting answers to which I relate.

Crystal Healing Therapy:
Using Crystals to Support Us On Our Road to Wellness

In our history, the use of crystals and stones for healing, protection, good luck, bringing prosperity, and many other purposes is greatly documented. Kings and queens adorned their crowns with them, warriors mounted them in their armor and shields, and alchemists used them to create healing tonics for their patients. Stones and crystals have been revered as helpers, and their specific purposes have been identified and cataloged by many. Though we are tempted to attribute the information to folk tales

> **"Crystals have their own vibration. When we touch crystals, we cause them to release their signature energy."**

and superstitions handed down through the ages, there are many that have taken a serious look at crystals as healing tools.

To understand Crystal Healing, we must be familiar with some facts about crystals and people. Let's talk about crystals first. Crystals, particularly quartz, have a crystalline structure. This structure allows them to amplify the energy around them by absorbing and reflecting it back out. This energy will affect objects and people near by. This is the basic principle for programming crystals

and using them as healing tools. Crystals also have their own vibration. When we touch crystals, we cause them to release their signature energy. This is called the piezoelectric effect. Just as we are all unique, each crystal has its own vibration. It is this "identity" that we intuitively or subconsciously tune into when coming in contact with a crystal. If the vibration of a crystal is useful to us, we will find it more attractive than another.

Crystals have been used both in their natural state and as carved cabochon or spheres as tools for healing, divining (gaining intuitive information), and as amplifiers for electronics.

When crystals were forming during the early stages of the Earth's development, they became "contaminated" with the elements around them. These elements gave the crystals color and properties that we can use to help us with specific needs. For example, Amethyst is a purple quartz, and it is known to ease temperaments and strengthen our immune systems.

Crystals that form in clumps and clusters have many pointed appendages. These are called points and are indeed pointed at one end and rough at the other end.

This shape compels the energy to flow in one direction, from the flat end up and out the pointed end. This type of crystal is used as a wand for focusing and moving energy, very much like a

---

"Humans, like all of nature, are free flowing with energy patterns that tell a story about who they are, where they have been . . . "

---

laser. You have to be careful with wands. The action of the wand is indiscriminate about the energy it moves. It just moves it. When using a wand on anyone, you will want to be very aware of the results of the focused energy. Both overloading or removing too much vital energy could have ill effects.

The energy pattern from rounded or smoothed crystals is more cyclic in nature. A crystal shaped as a sphere has no beginning or end, so the energy flows from its entire surface inward concentrating it and then sending it outward in all directions. The energy is experienced as a gentle cycling rather than a direct beam. This allows the individual to become balanced in the area where the sphere is placed. A rounded crystal also acts as a reflecting amplifier for the body and mind. This is especially beneficial when bringing forward negative subconscious programming to be released. There are applications for both kinds of crystals. Let your intuition guide you.

Humans, like all of nature, are free flowing with energy patterns that tell a story about who they are, where they have been, and what has

influenced them. These energy patterns cause discomfort when they become stagnant or out of sync with the natural vibration of the body. There are many effective ways to clear and harmonize the energy field around our bodies, and we can use crystals to support us as we heal.

What the heck is an energy field, you ask? We are all made up of layers of energy that vibrate at different frequencies. To give you a perspective of the whole picture, we sort of look like the rings found inside a tree. The human body is the core at the center of our being, and it vibrates the slowest. It is the only layer within our visual range. The rest of the layers vibrate beyond our physical vision. These layers are known as our aura (energy field).

"We are all made up of layers of energy that vibrate at different frequencies . . . like the rings found inside a tree."

The next two layers are the inner etheric and the etheric double. They hold the blueprint for the physical body and the energy to keep it all together. The next layer is the vital body. This is where we store the energy that supplies our physical body. Beyond the vital body is the astral layer. This is where we store our emotions and memories both conscious and unconscious. Now we come to the lower and higher mental layers. The lower mind is filled with your own thoughts, ideas and logical processes, while the higher mind takes you right to universal wisdom. The final layer is the spiritual body.

This is where we experience our connection to the universe in a very personal way. Though this is said to be the outer layer of our aura, who's to say it doesn't keep on going until we reach our source, but that is for another time.

Our aura spans about three feet around our physical bodies, but it has the capability to stretch much further. We also have seven major energy centers called chakras along a path or channel that goes down the center of our bodies from the top of our head to the end of our spinal column. The chakras receive and process information about the world around us. They also project information and feelings about us out into the world. It is in these layers of the aura

---

"A crystal can hold many programs, even if they are conflicting. They will hold onto the energy released by you."

---

and chakras that we form blocks that inhibit the healthy flow of our energy or life force. Left alone, they can manifest as physical conditions and diseases.

We use crystals and gemstones to amplify, absorb, transmute, move, or receive energy. Crystals are naturally harmonized to the human body and are easily programmed to work with the various vibrations found there. Using your mind or intent to program a crystal, you can work with it to directly influence the energy patterns held in your energy field.

To program a crystal, hold it in the palm of your right hand, and cradle your right hand in your left hand. By

doing this, you have completed the circuit and are connected to the consciousness of the crystal. Now, state your intention out loud to the crystal. It may sound something like this: "you will bring love and balance to my energy field for healing." Be clear and direct, because you are also programming your subconscious to receive the amplified message the crystal will be projecting. You may then choose to meditate with your crystal, carry it in your pocket, or keep it nearby during a healing session or doctor's appointment.

When you are done working with the crystal, give it a rest, and then clear it. Again, hold it in your hands and direct it to clear itself of all previous information. The clearing is enhanced by direct sunlight. You can also clear a crystal by running it under warm water. It is important to clear your crystals because it will continue to hold and transmit its programming until it's given new instructions. A crystal can hold many programs, even if they are conflicting. They will also hold onto the energy released by you. So, if it was unpleasant, you'll want to clear it.

Crystals can also be used to help you clear and balance your chakras. Choosing the proper crystal for each chakra is based on intuition and suggestions from others. It's helpful to know the color of each chakra since many times the best crystal to use is one that is the same color. The crown chakra on top of your head is violet. The third eye chakra is in the center of your forehead between your eyes and is indigo. Your throat chakra is blue. Your heart chakra is green, and the solar plexus, located over your stomach, is yellow. Your navel chakra is two inches below your belly button and is orange. Finally, the root chakra at the base of your spine is red. Many let the color of the chakra guide their crystal choices. For example, you may choose an Amethyst for the crown chakra because it is purple and has a strong affinity for spiritual concepts. But, if you find yourself feeling dizzy or getting a spinning sensation you may need a crystal that promotes grounding. Grounding is a term used to demonstrate the ability to be down to earth, focused, and in the present moment.

Some guidelines to follow are to know the properties of the stone you wish to use and pay attention to how you feel when it is in your field. Quartz crystals intensify and focus energy. They come in many colors and can be matched to many of the chakras easily. Fluorites also come in many colors. They absorb energy and have a very grounding and calming effect on the chakras. They are especially useful with emotional and physical discomforts. Calcite brings a feeling of peace and has the ability to remove pain. It is very soothing and comforting. It comes in many colors and can be used on any chakra.

Crystals, gemstones, and just plain ole river stones are all part of the vast mineral family that can be used as healing tools. If you are interested in learning more about this subject, go to the metaphysical section in your favorite book store.

Some of the books I've enjoyed are:

Love is in the Earth
by Melody

Crystal Healing, The Next Step
by Phyllis Galde

The Crystal Handbook
by Kevin Sullivan

Gemisphere Luminary
by Michael Katz.

Crystals for Healing

Clear Quartz wand

**Amethyst,
Citrine and Clear points**

Rose Quartz

Fluorite

Blue Calcite

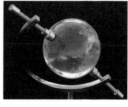

Quartz sphere

I Empower Myself

One of the more challenging lessons in my life was to feel empowered. To fully understand exactly what it meant to be empowered, I had to do research.

My first assignment was to study people I considered healthy, self-assured, confident risk-takers. I had to know what set them apart. Of course they had fears, but how did they overcome them? Also, where did their enthusiasm come from? I saw a joy in them that seemed to fuel their

---

"Through criticism, setbacks, and even failures, their own opinion of themselves was unshakable."

---

momentum to continue. I witnessed these people believe in themselves no matter what happened. Through criticism, setbacks, and even failures, their own opinion of themselves was unshakable or at worst needed just a little time to recover.

Next, I explored my own attitudes. How did I see myself? Did I feel like I had a place in this world? How did I feel about the people around me? What did I get excited about? Did I believe that I deserved . . . anything? A picture began to form in my mind. I saw a woman with dreams and desires for herself but too repressed

with anger, fear, jealousy, and other self-denying attitudes to feel free to act on her impulses.

How I came to be this woman is the story of my slumber. How I came to feel, be, and act empowered is the story of my healing and awakening.

In fact, my first experience of empowerment felt like waking up. It went something like this.

"I became aware that I was sleeping, then I fought to stay asleep, but then the morning light pushed through my eyelids, and I was awake. I slowly moved past the desire to continue sleeping and into curiosity about what was to happen next. Questions began to form in my mind. What will I do today? How will I accomplish my goals? What will get in my way? How will I handle that? I began to embrace the action of my life. I felt willing to participate. This is where it got tricky, because a part of me was also saying, don't go out there, there is failure, rejection, embarrassment, and who knows what else. It's just not worth all the pain. Give up . . . "

It took an act of self-empowerment to overcome this negative chatter. All the warnings were based on old programming that believed I am weak and can't make "good for me" decisions or I won't be able to handle objections and rejections.

When I empower myself, I give myself permission to feel my feelings, work through them, and go forward toward my goal. When I empower myself, I am gentle with my fears and forgiving of my mistakes. I am my own best friend. I give myself the best possible advice and boost my esteem with words of encouragement. I also used the "fake it until you make it" plan for a while. I had to prove I was strong before I believed I was strong. Eventually, I got in touch with most of the fears that kept me inferior to my real self, dealt with them, and no longer needed to fake a powerful me. I was a powerful me. Fear can be an ominous opponent. When we believe in the strength of our fear and the weakness of ourselves, we pull our own plug.

I wasn't always successful in willing myself into greatness. When I fell, I reached out for help. Eve Wilson, my spiritual teacher, guided me to join with the energy of animals to act as surrogate powerhouses for me while I developed the needed strength and resolve within myself. An excerpt from Eve's Healer Development Training Manual explains this phenomenon.

"Fear can be an ominous opponent. When we believe in the strength of our fear and the weakness of ourselves, we pull our own plug"

"Power Animals bring their unique gifts and strengths to a person as a spiritual or soul medicine to awaken the power within an individual, allowing them to be empowered, to move forward in their lives, and to heal in ways which seemed impossible prior

to the power animal retrieval."

The retrieval process is performed with a trained healer or shaman and is done through a meditative journey. Once the Power Animal is discovered, it is "blown" into your heart and crown chakras. Then you merge with the animal by imitating its sounds and movements while drumming softly. The more you allow yourself to be the power animal, the deeper you merge with it. When I did this in a group session, we sounded like a day at the zoo. It was great fun. I was amazed to see everyone receive the exact animal they needed.

"The more you allow yourself to be the power animal, the deeper you merge with it."

This month we will work with Anna, the Goddess of Empowerment. Through her message and meditation you will learn to look within, connect with your personal power and begin living your life from this place. She will also guide you toward identifying and healing each resistance you have to being a self-assured, confident person.

Another aspect of self-empowerment comes within the expression of our sexuality. Unblocking self-love opens doors to loving others in a full and complete way. Stacy Theodossin enlightens us with some tantalizing advice about heightening love between two people. Tantra is the ancient practice of lovemaking that elevates a physical experience to a spiritual union. I invite you to read about tantra and bring sensuality back into sexuality.

November

I Empower Myself

Some Things To Do This Month

When overcoming an illness, meditate and visualize yourself healthy and rejoining your life with gusto.

To increase your stamina, picture yourself standing in the center of a ball of orange light. Feel it enliven you and bring joy to your heart.

Feel the courageous energy around you and become someone's hero (even for yourself).

Living With Moon Energy

The Moon is the closest heavenly body to our planet. Her affect on us is real and immediate. Tracking the phases of the Moon and the zodiac sign she is traveling through can map out a cause and effect cycle for us. It will help make sense of our mood swings and patterns of luck, both good and bad.

Look up the Moon table on page 151 and record the date and zodiac sign the New and Full Moons are in.

Next, write down how you felt the three days around the New and Full Moons. Also record what was happening in your life at these times. Keeping track of this information will help you anticipate and prepare for future influences from the Moon. You may also compare your life with the interpretations provided on page 148.

Notes on how the energy of the New Moon and Full Moon affect me.

November's Goddess

To empower is to authorize. When we empower ourselves, we are simply giving ourselves permission to follow our hearts. On paper, this looks easy enough, but I hear your wheels turning. From experience, we have learned that empowered behavior takes more than finesse and the right attitude. We really have to be prepared emotionally and mentally. Based on what we learned in the 70's, when empowerment was called assertiveness, we still can't be bullies. Powerful is not the same as power over. Nor can we pretend we are empowered, for our fear will swiftly pull the rug out from underneath us. In the following meditation, you will go on a journey with the goddess Anna. She will help you remove the blocks to becoming empowered and teach you the truth about living in your power.

Meditation: You will need an orange candle and a clear quartz crystal point. Prepare for your meditation in a comfortable and familiar way. Review previous meditations if you need to and be sure to connect with the Earth and your creator to anchor you. Once you feel relaxed and your candle is lit, close your eyes and state your intention to connect with the goddess Anna. Then, begin to imagine an orange light emanating from your second chakra, which is two inches below you navel. Let your consciousness (mind) flow down into your second chakra and be in the center of this orange light. When you feel completely anchored there, look up and see another orange light coming toward you. It stops a short distance before you and sends you a message that it is Anna. Once you feel confident that you are in the presence of Anna, begin building a bridge of light to her. When it is done, invite her to cross the bridge and visit with you in your room of orange light. It is here where you will ask Anna to show you a block that prevents you from feeling and being empowered. Ask her to teach you how to heal this situation, and follow her instructions. Then, ask Anna to show you how you would have acted if you were already living as an empowered being. Now, hold the crystal point at heart level in front of you. Ask Anna to program the crystal with the energy of the learned behavior. Later, you can carry it with you and let it beam this energy back to you. As a note: if you find there is something you are not ready to do, promise to look at it another time and ask that the situation be closed for now.

If you desire to work with another block, ask Anna to reveal it and begin the process again. When you are done healing as many blocks as you wish, take a moment to let all the teachings settle in. Allow Anna to bring the healing into your body, mind, and spirit. After a period of time, you will feel complete with this meditation. Release Anna with gratitude, and return your attention to the room you are in. Take a deep cleansing breath and become fully awake. Record your experience in your journal.

Anna *Goddess of Empowerment*

Deep within you is a seed of life that is powerfully focused and dedicated to success. It knows only of the love and excitement of creation and the expression of its desires. This seed is the driving force behind taking charge of your life and living it according to your plan.

I am Anna, the Goddess of Empowerment, and I support you in your need to tap into the energy of personal power. I will help you harness this primal energy and develop the skills needed to work with it. I will teach you how to connect and merge with this seed of life and act as one. In this union, you will feel more like getting into the game and less like standing on the sidelines. In fact, you may feel like creating a game of your own.

Watch your own progress as the merging with this seed of life dissolves the fears that held you back from being empowered and guides you back onto your path with renewed strength and enthusiasm.

Let me be the wind beneath your wings that take you to the heights attainable when you empower yourself.

Know courage by attempting the impossible on your own.

I empower myself

Capture a moment that has brought you a smile or giggle; stretch it out, then step into it. Feel it with your whole being, and experience "Lightening up."

Sacred Sensuality:
An Introduction to Tantra
By Stacy Theodossin

We are all cerebral, emotional, spiritual, sensual, and sexual beings. We are a union of body, mind, and spirit. These qualities exist in each of us from conception. However, societal and cultural mores often place restrictions on our sensuality. Sexuality and sensuality are viewed as sinful or hedonistic, something that should not be talked about or expressed openly. Society asks that we separate the "inappropriate" parts of ourselves. Through complying with these limitations, we are no longer whole.

Tantra seeks to integrate all of these qualities that make us total beings. In tantric practice, sexuality and spirituality are not separate, they are undeniably intertwined.

"Tantra is about emotional sharing and intimacy. It's more important to show who you really are rather than be concerned with sexual technique."

Tantra, as a spiritual practice, can be traced back to the 5th Century. This Eastern tradition reached its peak in the 1200s. However, it still remains a prominent part of Indian culture and ritual. Renewed interest in tantra has been on the rise for the past several

years and is currently making its mark in Western culture.

Our culture has often looked for immediate gratification - in our lives, business dealings, and intimate relationships. Tantric union, however, should be savored as a sumptuous banquet. Sensuality should not be rushed like so many other areas of our lives.

There are many aspects of sensuality and sexuality to be explored in tantra. However, it is important to remember that the only goal of tantra is to be completely in the moment with your partner, relishing your experience. Tantra is about emotional sharing and intimacy. It is more important to share who you really are rather than being concerned with sexual technique. Tantra is concerned with acceptance and embracing the sensory experience. You surrender, consciously, to the moment. When we do this, we transcend the world of attachment. We allow our feelings to flow, which allows us to develop empathy for our lovers and ourselves. Through this sharing, we can deepen our intimacy with our lover.

Tantra is a Sanskrit word meaning balanced union of opposite poles. These polarities are Shiva, the male energy, and Shakti, the female energy. When these two polarities come together in tantric union, they allow for a meditative liberation of mind and body. Through this liberation, a couple can reach a higher consciousness or higher spirituality together.

With tantra, it is important to create sacred space. When you are entertaining special dinner guests, you want to make your home look beautiful and inviting. You would set the table with china, crystal, linen napkins, flowers, and candles. Just as you would set the mood and ambience for a special dinner, you should create a sanctuary for tantric exploration with your lover. With tantra, you want to embrace all of the senses. Presence, ambience, touch, taste, fragrance, tone, color, and form all play factors in setting the sacred space for this connection. Some things that create a pleasing environment are soft music, candles, a fire, an alluring fragrance from flowers or incense, and a comfortable place to relax. Once the sacred space has been created, invite your lover to share it with you.

The "Secret Garden Ceremony" can be a good way to connect with your lover and establish intimacy, once the sacred space has been created. In this ceremony, the recipient is to receive without giving back. When your lover is receptive, they have a choice to be present, without expectation. When creating this space, it is important to have no attachments to the outcome of your actions. Although the union may result in sexual intercourse, that is never the goal. Let go of all of your judgments,

and let your lover be just exactly who they are. Just being in the moment and connecting with your lover is all that is important. When your lover is open and receptive, and you are both feeling connected, it is an ideal time to lavish them with special attention. This is a good time to feed, bath, or massage your lover.

"In Tantric union, it is important to allow adequate time for arousal, at least an hour or two"

All of these sensual pleasures reinforce your special connection with each other. Just allow your lover to enjoy all the sensations. In tantric union, it is important to allow adequate time for arousal, at least an hour or two. Remember this is a feast, not a take-out meal.

When feeding your lover, present a platter that will arouse a visual feast. Fruits, nuts, cheeses, chocolate, and breads all make pleasing combinations. Make sure that each food has a wonderful aroma, taste, texture, and color. As you feed your lover, use your fingers. Allow your lover to close their eyes and slowly savor all of the unique flavors. Allow them to feel and sense the foods. Have your lover inhale the scent of each food; rub each food on their lips -- to give them a hint of what is to come. Don't hurry! Let the moments linger between each nibble. You may also want to provide something to quench your lover's thirst. Fruit juices, wine, or champagne add to the decadence of this ceremony. Allow some of the liquid to caress their lips and skin.

Feeding your lover can even be combined with the tantric bath ritual. When bathing your lover, be prepared for all of their needs in advance. Have the tub filled with warm water, fragrant oils and/or rose petals. Place candles or incense around the room to make an inviting atmosphere - before you even lead them to the space. Have a ladle available to pour warm water over them as they relax into the tub. Just allow the water and the scents to envelop their body and comfort them for as long as they like. Have soft, fresh towels available and dry your lover off when they come out of the tub. Take care of their every need so that they feel completely loved.

If you want to prolong the arousal time, massage is always a good way to connect further with your lover. Offer to delicately massage their body with fragrant oils. Ask them where they want to be massaged. This will relax and arouse your lover even further. At this time, you and your lover may want to give to each other mutually. Eye gazing is a great way to connect on a soul level and deepens your intimacy.

Your tantric connection can end after sharing these sensual delights. Or, if you are in the mood for dessert, they may continue.

It is important for the female energy (Shakti) to rise from the root chakra where the kundalini resides. Chakras are energy centers that reside in specific areas of the body. A woman's sexual energy is drawn up from the root chakra (base of the spine) and should be pulled into the heart chakra, in the center of the chest. The male energy (Shiva) is drawn down from the crown or head chakra until it meets the female energy in his heart chakra. Once both Shiva and Shakti energies are residing in the heart chakras, you will both feel universal love. Once this heart connection is established, this is a good time to

---

"Once both Shiva and Shakti energies are residing in the heart chakras, you will both feel universal love"

---

continue with your tantric exploration of each other.

Tantra is a beautiful union of ritual, sensuality, and spirituality. It is meant to draw you and your lover closer as you explore each other and really take your time to connect spiritually and sensually, not just sexually. Each moment of your union should be savored, never rushed. Your only goal is to really connect with your lover in a receptive and open environment. Enjoy!

Stacy Theodossin is an Ayurvedic Healer and Reiki Practitioner. Stacy lives and works in Dearborn, Michigan. email: healinggoddess@aol.com.

This is Who I Am

I like saying that. This is who I am. It satisfies the need in me to have sound identity and purpose in my life. I feel control and strength flow through my veins. I picture myself standing on top of a mountain with the wind in my hair, arms stretched out and yelling "this is who I am, and I like it. And I don't care if you don't." Whew, I'm glad I got that out of my system. Using my identity aggressively has got to be annoying, not to mention potentially dangerous to my fellow humankind. I have to maintain that I can be myself without hitting others over the head with it.

"I feel strong but not poised for battle. I feel free because I have just given the world and all its inhabitants back to themselves."

I know what motivated me to be so dramatic about who I am. I doubt myself. I have insecurities about my thoughts and feelings. If they get me in trouble, I don't want to own them. If they bring me praise and admiration, I may reject them. Truthfully, this is not who I am. This is who I act like when I am afraid of my power.

Being empowered means making a commitment to myself to act like a grown-up. It means acting responsible. It means responding to life - my life. It means standing on that mountaintop calmly declaring "this is who I am, and I like it. It suits me, and it only has to suit me." I am able to live my life, confident that I will take care of my business and step aside to make room for others to take care of theirs. I feel strong but not poised for battle. I feel free because I have just given the world and all its inhabitants back to themselves. I let loose all the entanglements that confuse the boundaries of my individuality and theirs. I am only responsible for myself, and I define my identity within that parameter. This is a kinder, gentler manifestation of my being.

Oh, but what about the children, the elderly, the sick, the poor, the environment? Someone has to be responsible for them. This is where I demonstrate who I am. I choose whom I will help, and my actions are an outward expression of what I know about myself inside. I will be honest about my abilities and willingness. I will act from that and not from a place of false modesty where misplaced intentions could cause someone to get hurt.

All the work from the previous months has led us up to this moment. We have set the foundation to feel free to show the world "this is who I am" by calling our hurt parts home through understanding and forgiveness. We have explored our gifts and talents, and we've given ourselves permission to express them. We have taken steps to feel more empowered in our daily lives.

Now, do you feel ready to stand up and declare this is who I am? Are you ready to see your true identity in the things you do? Does saying out loud "this is who I am" give you a full feeling of joy and strength? If not, clarify it for yourself. Make new choices. Let every action, thought, and word demonstrate who you have discovered yourself to be. Then, ask yourself, what is left to do? What part of me is crying out, "I just can't risk it, there is just too much to lose", or that just doesn't feel like me? Then, compassionately love those parts of you. They are frightened, judged, and misunderstood. They speak of a time when you acted from a place of courage and were thwarted. They remember, and they need help evolving up and out to join you as the person you are now and aspire to be.

Katelyn, the Goddess of Individuality, is waiting to take you to a place of liberation and delightful satisfaction.

It is where you release and transform the layers of false identity placed over the real you. She is the embodiment of renewed life emerging from the power that being an individual brings. When participating in Katelyn's meditation, ask to be guided toward connecting with your true identity so you can manifest it throughout your life in a way that serves you and brings you fulfillment.

"Let every action, thought, and word demonstrate who you have discovered yourself to be."

We wrap this year up with an article on "Creating Meaningful Ritual in Our Life" by Jacki Smith. Jacki's life is rich with ritual, and she gives us some insight into how to do this for ourselves. Finally, she wrote a couple of great rituals for us to participate in. You can use them as a formula for creating a ritual unique to your own life.

Thank you for joining me on this year-long journey into self-discovery. I hope it introduced you to yourself and some new and promising ways to heal your life.

Patty Shaw

Bridget *by Jacki Smith*

I felt you today,
You filled my spirit
  with your presence.

I felt you today,
Your flames lapped over my skin
  gentle heat surrounded me
While your fire cleansed my spirit

I felt you today
  as your garden called to me

My mind traveled there and I was strengthened.
I felt you today,
Reminding me
  that you have always been with me

I saw you today
  when I was reflected in the mirror
And I knew
  the power that lays in my hands
  and the responsibility you left to me

Today I know you.

December

This is who I am

Some Things To Do This Month

Share your talents with others, and experience fulfillment.

Building your immune system will help you stay vibrant for the winter ahead. Learn everything you can about what your body needs to stay healthy.

Take up a cause you believe in, and compassionately demonstrate your abilities.

Living With Moon Energy

The Moon is the closest heavenly body to our planet. Her affect on us is real and immediate. Tracking the phases of the Moon and the zodiac sign she is traveling through can map out a cause and effect cycle for us. It will help make sense of our mood swings and patterns of luck, both good and bad.

Look up the Moon table on page 151 and record the date and zodiac sign the New and Full Moons are in.

Next, write down how you felt the three days around the New and Full Moons . Also record what was happening in your life at these times. Keeping track of this information will help you anticipate and prepare for future influences from the Moon. You may also compare your life with the interpretations provided on page 148.

Notes on how the energy of the New Moon and Full Moon affect me.

December's Goddess

We all need a nudge to get out there and be ourselves. Many of us are not comfortable acting on the impulses of our uniqueness. We get caught up in what others will think of us. There is a kind of safety in saying and doing what is acceptable. The consequence is the sellout feeling we have to live with. Then, on comes the cloak of illusion, and pretty soon we start forgetting who we are and identify with the cloak. We look in the mirror and either believe the false face or grieve for the face we covered up. In this meditation, Katelyn will take you on a journey to meet your true essence. There, you will be given an opportunity to choose again. Will you still need to keep things the way they are, or are you ready to drop the false identity and begin again?

Meditation: You will need a yellow candle and a mirror. Light the candle and prepare for your meditation by connecting to the Earth and the creator or source as described in the earlier months. Invite your spirit helpers to be with you and support you during this journey.

Once you feel comfortable and relaxed, let your consciousness travel into your heart. Imagine a beautiful gate before you. Open the gate, and enter into the most magnificent place you have ever been. Scan the space with your eyes, and notice a woman sitting off in the distance. Once she knows you've become aware of her, she rises and walks toward you. This is Katelyn.

After a warm greeting, tell Katelyn that you are here to meet your true essence and would like her help. She explains to you that your true essence is the state of being of your brand new soul. It had not yet been imprinted with the beliefs created out of your reactions to your experiences.

Katelyn asks you to close your eyes and begin the journey back to the moment of separation. When you arrive, observe yourself with as many senses as possible. Allow yourself to feel what you were feeling as a new soul. If the separation caused you pain in any way, you will need a healing. Allow Katelyn to heal your soul in every way needed. Once the healing is complete, connect with your soul again and learn about yourself. Ask questions, receive information, and revel in the freshness you feel. When you are done, let the essence of your soul seep into you and reprogram all the changes made in you over time. Ask that this healing be brought forward through all of your experiences into the present.

When that is complete, talk with Katelyn about all the ways you have not acted as your true self. She will reveal your motivation and what you had to lose or gain. With this new level of honesty, you can wake with the knowing of who you are and how you will express it. Thank Katelyn, slowly return to your body and the room, and say aloud the date and time. Open your eyes and look into the mirror and see who looks back. Write it all down.

Katelyn

Goddess of Individuality

I am Katelyn, and there is no other like me. I express my individuality proudly, without hesitation or apology. My strength comes from the knowledge that I am unique even though I may look like you. This is a quiet power, felt deep within. I draw upon it to achieve my many accomplishments

I value my existence, and I know that the contributions of my life force are instrumental to the continuation of the cycles of creation. I do not question my worth, but honor it as a gift for my benefit as well as everyone else's.

It is my goal to bring you down the path of your life to a place that reminds you of the unique individual that you are. There you will experience your beginning and recall why you have come into being.

I will show you the many cloaks of illusion you wear. I will help you gain confidence in yourself so you can begin shedding those cloaks to reveal the truth. The truth of you.

We all await your rebirth and the expression of the original intention of your soul. When you are ready, show us, tell us who you are.

I stand here waiting to bask in the glory of you. Let me see your light and join you in the celebration of your unique individuality.

Katelyn **139**

D E C E M B E R

Pass on cherished wisdom that has made your life easier.

This is who I am

She wears flowers, for they mirror the ones in her soul.

D E C E M B E R

Manifestation is a game of creation.
The tools are motivation, desire, and passion.

Creating Meaningful Ritual in Our Life

By Jacki Smith

The word Ritual conjures up images ranging from a Catholic mass to a few witches gathered around a candle calling in the elements with an upraised athame, wand, bowl of salt, and chalice of water. Yet, we can re-write the word ritual to mean the repeating actions in our lives that empower and focus our intentions.

We ritualize many aspects of our lives, possibly not realizing what level of importance they play and how deep they go. The simple task of waking up in the morning is built upon years of ritual. When we deviate from that path, it is a simple statement of "getting up on the wrong side of the bed" that reminds us of how imbedded into our psyche this morning ritual is. Other lifestyle rituals may include the routine of coming home from work, Saturday house cleaning, bill paying, or even how you mow the lawn. Many superstitions are personal rituals used to clear away intruding negative thoughts: "knock wood, a purse on the floor, or a pinch of salt over your back." All of these statements take the feeling of "bad" luck and transform it into "good" luck.

You can design a custom ritual to promote healing, create clarity, or co-ordinate the efforts of a group into one collective intention. Include elements that represent the body, mind, and spirit, or the conscious & subconscious, or the waking and dreaming worlds, or the five senses and intuition, or the four elements of life: air, fire, water and earth. The point is to include the physical and non-physical aspects of life in your ritual.

This multi-level ritual teaches your psyche about the new intention and reality you are creating, which aligns you with this new essence. All you

---

"We ritualize many aspects of our lives, possibly not realizing what level of importance they play and how deep they go."

---

need to do is relax and let it touch upon all your senses.

See it: have a focal point to focus on.

Hear it: speak your intention aloud, continuing to repeat it until you memorize it.

Smell it: use a pleasing aroma, incense, or candle to create a memory path that you may easily call upon.

Touch it: have a talisman or touch-stone to carry with you as a reminder of your healing.

Taste it: a small glass of wine, juice, or tea to fully ingest this new essence you are creating.

Remember, in creating a ritual, keeping it simple keeps it powerful. Below you will find two sample rituals to use as a basis for creating your own. The first one is a ritual before you eat. It reinforces the belief that whatever food you eat will nourish you and keep you healthy. The second ritual is one for healing.

Food Blessing Ritual

Before you consume any meal, snack, or drink, remember that you are made up of divine energy, and so is the food and drink you are about to consume. No matter what the ingredients, all of them have originated from the Earth and were originally designed by nature to sustain, fulfill, and heal the body.

Take a brief moment to silently thank the Earth for the nourishment you are about to receive. Remind yourself that this sustenance that you are about to put in your mouth is full of healthy energy and brings fulfillment to your body, mind, and spirit. Lastly, thank yourself for being healthy and nurturing to yourself.

Healing Ritual

Find a quiet place where you will be undisturbed for at least 30 to 60 minutes. Bring with you:

- Clean loose paper and pencil
- Candle, dim light or mirror
- Incense and burner or your favorite essential oil

- A piece of jewelry or tumbled stone,
- Wine or juice and a glass

Sit comfortably, and declare that this room you are in is a sacred space filled with healing energy. All negative and unnecessary energy is now cleared from the room, and you are ready to begin your healing journey.

Now relax and clear your mind by allowing it to drift. Gently release any thoughts that enter, and allow your mind to clear itself of the stress and clutter of the day.

"It reinforces the belief that whatever food you eat will nourish you and keep you healthy."

Once you are fully relaxed, write your intention for healing on your piece of paper. Keep all phrases positive and healing. For example:

"Fill my body, mind, and spirit with healing energy. I release what is troubling me to the transformative powers of (God, the Universe, my guardian/healing angel, the Earth, the Goddess, etc). My dis-ease leaves my (body, mind, or spirit), and I manifest health in all of its forms."

Then on the opposite side of the paper, write what is troubling you. Use as much detail as possible.

Light the candle / dim light or look deeply into your own eyes in the mirror. Light the incense, and allow the smoke to encompass your whole being. -OR- Anoint the crown of your head, the middle of your forehead, your throat, the middle of your chest, your solar plexus, your knees, and the bottom of your feet with the essential oils. Hold the jewelry or stone in one hand, and touch your filled glass with the other.

Say aloud the intention that you wrote, repeating it until you no longer need to look at the paper, then repeat it several more times.

Stare deeply into the flame of the candle or at your own eyes in the mirror. Continue repeating the intention in your thoughts until your entire mind is focused there. You will now feel your body change density.

You will now feel either lighter or heavier, yet filled with a new energy. Flow with this feeling, filling yourself completely and allowing your essence to transform. Feel it flow through your trunk, arms, legs, feet, and hands. Feel the flow through your hands and into what you are holding.

Feel this energy flow down your legs, carrying the dis-ease out of your body, through your feet, and into the earth. The earth welcomes this energy, for she is a natural filter willing to transform this energy into healing energy as it passes through her core.

Once you feel completely filled and all energy has been flowing through you for a while, slowly, easily rebalance

your energy, not too much and not too little, releasing the energy that you do not need. Slowly bring your awareness back to your surroundings and re-center your mind in the present here and now. Lift your glass, give thanks to your higher power for this miracle of healing, and drink down all of what fills your glass.

As you go forward in life, carry with you the piece of jewelry or stone that you energized. Every time your attention goes to that object, repeat your intention silently to yourself and know that the healing continues.

Filling your life with these little rituals and moments of thanks will continue to heal and empower your life, bringing you to a higher state of consciousness.

Bright Blessings in all that you do and remember the seeds of magic are found in your imagination and planted in your deeds.

 Jacki Smith is the founder of Coventry Creations, Inc, a poet and gives seminars on personal empowerment and Candle Magic.

She can be reached at (248) 545-8360.

Find her candles on the internet at www.coventrycreations.com

Goddess Mother
by Jacki Smith

Rising sun
    you lift my soul
Dancing light
    fills my lungs
      with hues of inspiration

Your wisdom dances
    through nature
Teaching
    the most delicate flower
    and the toughest blade of grass
    how to reach
      for your caress

Articles continued . . .

January-"Everything That was Old" . . .

belief in yourself. With a feeling of gratitude, make a pact with this angel to quietly remove the new contract and head back to heaven once you have grown past the need for it.

Once this is complete, thank Archangel Michael for his help in this healing, and trust that support is there for you as you grow and develop in this area of your life. Release yourself out of this meditation with a few deep-cleansing breaths and call yourself back into the room by wiggling your toes and stretching. Drink a little water to ground you in the present. If you still feel fuzzy headed, sit down and imagine a white glowing shadow of yourself settling down into your body connecting with you from your feet up to the top of your head, and welcome yourself home.

Meditating with creative visualizations is very effective for making positive changes in our lives and improving the quality of our energy.

What would you say if I told you of a therapy that gets the same and even better results with the touch of your own finger to accupressure points on your own body? Return to page 12 to read about Stephen Daniel and Quantum Techniques. Learn how this cutting edge tool can identify and correct disrupted emotional, mental, physical, and spiritual vibrations in our body and return to us our health, vitality, and passion for life.

February-"Still Cleaning up" . . .

things much longer than is good for me as if I've developed huge pinching claws. My hard shell, well, it's there and causes me to be misunderstood, and even unapproachable at times.

These three qualities have contributed to the development of a defense system the military couldn't infiltrate. The reality of that is, if nothing can get in, nothing can get out. That is why it's so important for me to keep cleaning up the mess I made last year. This shell is only so big, and I have to let some things go by using forgiveness, surrender, and love so I can maintain my commitment to my health, happiness, and my perfect size 12 shell.

We all have to make choices, and some of them are very difficult. Lets' learn from the crab and develop our discernment about when to hold onto something and when to let go. When to let someone inspire us and when to say, not for me, thank you very much. When to stand and face our challenges and when to retreat to think it over. I have a friend who can help you while you develop your discernment muscle. Her name is Meredith, the Goddess of Balance.

A balanced perspective is crucial in decision making. When you are too emotional or lack some important information to make a clear solid decision, call on the Goddess Meredith to assist you. She offers a message and a meditation to guide you when it's time to make decisions. You may find you knew the right answer all along, but isn't it nice to have a Goddess to support you and give insights to different possibilities.

The featured article for February discusses Chiropractic Medicine. Dr. Stacy Winn offers intelligent insights on health, quality of life, and how to maintain it with the aid of Chiropractic adjustments. I have had

Chiropractic treatments for different symptoms and have found them to be very beneficial. Tension, stress and overwork had locked my body up and caused pain. It was great to feel relief from the pain after an adjustment, but the greatest treat was feeling the energy move freely in my body again. Honestly, I felt a little younger. It is my hope that Dr. Stacy Winn opens another door for you as you build your repertoire of alternative healing modalities.

March-"Expressing Myself" ...

heal the blind spot in your soul that keeps you from knowing and expressing yourself and the gift or gifts you brought with you when you were born. Follow the meditation with the intention to discover your gifts and talents and wait patiently for an answer. Be loving and kind to yourself and appreciate yourself every step of the way as you grow and develop. Dedicate your March journal pages to documenting your awakening talents.

For inspiration, watch the movie *My Left Foot*. It is based on a true story about Christy Brown, a writer and artist born with cerebral palsy. He only has the use of his left leg, torso, and head. His struggle to express himself and be understood is remarkable. I see him as a teacher as well. His tenacity showed me that, when it comes to finding out what I am all about, never settle for another's definition of me.

Petra Schnieder and Gerhard Pieroth are two more courageous people that have faced their fears and committed their lives to developing a way for all of us to become who we are.

Featured in March's article on alternative therapies, Petra and Gerhard introduce to us the gift of working with Ascended Spiritual Masters, Archangels, and Earthangels. These beings teach us through their own mastery and gifts how to clear out what stops us from expressing our full potential and realizing the joy living on Earth can bring us. Along with the teachings and meditations, Petra and Gerhard present us with a concept called vibrational medicine. Through meditation and a gift for channeling, Petra and Gerhard captured the vibration of each Master or Angel and put it in oil. They call these oils Lightbeing essences, and when we keep the oil blends close to our bodies, our own energy field will be healed of blockages that have kept us stuck in negative ways.

There are 21 Master Essences, 8 Archangel Essences, 8 Earthangel Essences, and two books that describe the lesson each Lightbeing teaches. All products are available over the internet, and I highly recommend them. For a complete description of their work, see the article on Mastery in Life with Lightbeings Essences.

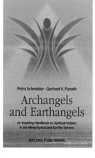

The Many Faces of the Moon

By Lisa Fryer

New Moon in Aries

The New Moon in Aries, ruled by Mars, heightens our sense of individuality. It shows us new ways to express ourselves and assert our true nature. It's time for a collective makeover, especially on our bodies. Aries is the "I AM" principal and calls us to get in touch with our Divine self.

Full Moon in Aries

The Full Moon in Aries sways us to assert our individuality, independence, and our sense of "I AM". Be careful not to butt heads or wage battle with anyone, especially a sweetheart. Everyone will be feeling his or her "oats". If feelings are in question, this Full Moon will inspire a better idea of where everyone stands.

New Moon in Taurus

The Taurus New Moon brings our attention to how we handle our money and what we want to commit our funds toward. This time will reflect our growing maturity and ability to share our abundance. A new budget needs to reflect changing needs. Nature is calling, so make plans for spending time outdoors.

Full Moon in Taurus

Full Moon in Taurus represents money, values, nature, and our material foundation. Whatever makes us feel secure will be rocked and challenged. The key is to become our own anchor and have a "phase two" in the big picture. Don't be attached to the form that security takes.

New Moon in Gemini

New Moon in Gemini gives us a sense of excitement and friendly communication. A zeal for information can send us back to school or into new research. Magic sparks when spiritual gifts are developed and shared.

Full Moon in Gemini

When the Full Moon is in the sign of Gemini, our communication skills are put to the test, and heavy issues may be overly intellectualized. Listen fully and intently, important matters will materialize and become resolved with those involved.

New Moon in Cancer

Creative Cancer hosts this New Moon, which also rules our deepest identity and what we think of as home. Spend lots of time cultivating a relationship with yourself, and what is held closest to the heart. Focus on developing more comfort at home, emotionally and aesthetically.

Full Moon in Cancer

The Full Moon in Cancer draws our attention to the ends of cycles. We may feel the nudge to finish cleaning that closet or making sure all family issues are dealt with. Whatever the case may be, it will evolve around the home, family, and health.

New Moon in Leo

Playful Leo energizes the Sun/Moon union. A powerful fiery romance is in the air, triggering the intensity of our hearts, so take courageous chances in love! A whole new, exciting freedom-oriented relationship is on the horizon. By empowering others, we empower ourselves! Leave others free, and so too will we be free.

Full Moon in Leo

The Full Moon in warm-hearted Leo will keep our social calendars busier than ever. The warm fuzzies have never been warmer and expressed more abundantly! This is a great time to go out and be seen and let our true bodacious colors show!

New Moon in Virgo

The Virgo New Moon asks us to reset our priorities to serve our highest purpose on our road toward enlightenment. We will see the results of our plan in action and realize helpful revisions. This is a great time to form new habits in regards to healing, organizing, and planning your next spiritual step.

Full Moon in Virgo

The Full Moon in service and detail oriented Virgo will shed light on ways we can be more of service to others and ourselves and catch up on some details we may have missed along the way. Organizing our priorities and path of self-healing leaves us ripe for upcoming romance and social opportunities.

New Moon in Libra

The New Moon in Libra, the sign of relationships, partnerships, and justice, infuses relationships with new beginnings. It also may be that we let go of partnerships that are co-dependent or unbalanced. If it's become a game of tug of war, let go of the rope! This is a time for wiping the slate clean and creating harmony.

Full Moon in Libra

Relationships come to their climactic or anti-climactic resolve with a Full Moon in Libra. Venus, the ruler of Libra, reminds us of our ideals concerning relationships, equality, justice, and sharing. Make a truly deeper connection. This energy helps us decide which lesson we are finishing and where to go from here.

New Moon in Scorpio

A Scorpio New Moon enables us to become aware of unhealthy patterns in our lives. Transformation is Scorpio's stellar job, so take advantage of the planetary opportunity that opens a door deep inside of our hidden desires, hopes, and dreams. Follow THAT star for a while!

Full Moon in Scorpio

The energy of the Full Moon in Scorpio brings us great strength and tenacity to finish what we started. Our survival skills will peak and be available at a moment's notice. We will tend to be a little more secretive, but that's ok, it all comes out in the wash eventually.

New Moon in Sagittarius

This New Moon in Sagittarius makes us aware of the excitement in the air. Today, anything becomes possible, there is joy in just being alive and human. Clearing out unnecessary vibrations will leave us free to adventure into the world or into the beauty of life and our own spirit.

Full Moon in Sagittarius

The Full Moon in Sagittarius, which rules philosophy, religion, and the "big picture", will make us become more aware of the ways we need to spread our wings and how we can fly. Watch as some of our grander schemes come together for closure.

New Moon in Capricorn

The New Moon in hard-working, organized, tenacious Capricorn shows us new ways of working more effectively. We all get a new start in strengthening the financial bottom line and injecting new dedication to our chosen career path.

Full Moon in Capricorn

Capricorn's Full Moon asks us to make compromises as far as work is concerned for healing on a greater scale. Some of us may decide to change our direction, perhaps to do it on our own. Follow your heart at work, and your career will bring you closer to your goals. If we act now, we keep our options open.

New Moon in Aquarius

The New Moon in inventive, inquisitive Aquarius brings us new inventions and innovative thinking. The timing is right to express the many ideas welling up inside of us now! Revelations are bountiful with a New Moon in exciting and unpredictable Aquarius. We can write our own rules!

Full Moon in Aquarius

The Aquarian Full Moon triggers our need for more freedom. This energy asks us to put our new ideas into practice. This will bring about unrealized hopes, wishes, and plans for all of us! Be prepared for others to say what is on their mind! Every man and woman is a star during an Aquarian moon. We all get to do our own thing, and let others do theirs!

New Moon in Pisces

The New Moon in mystical, intuitive Pisces opens new doors of higher consciousness around the world. It's a call to express our greatest compassion and love for those around us, especially for those who suffer more than we do.

Full Moon in Pisces

The Full Moon in Pisces intensifies everyone's psychic abilities and heightened awareness of subtle, subconscious energies that float around. Personal signs from the universe regarding what concerns us most will be more accessible. If you ask, it will answer.

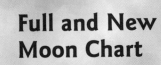

Full and New Moon Chart

	2008		2009		2010		2011		2012	
	NM	FM	NM	FM	NM	FM	NM	FM	NM	FM
January	8Cp	22Ca	26Aq	11Ca	15Cp	30Le	4Cp	19Ca	23Cp	19Ca
February	7Aq	21Le	25Pi	9Le	14Aq	28Le	3Cp	18Le	21Aq	7Le
March	7Pi	21Ge	26Pi	11Vi	15Pi	30Li	4Pi	19Vi	22Pi	8Vi
April	6Ar	20Li	25Ta	9Li	14Ar	28Sc	3Ar	18Li	21Ar	6Li
May	5Ta	20Sc	24 Ta	9Sc	14Ta	27Sc	3Ta	17Sc	20Ta	6Sc
June	3Ge	18Sg	24Ge	7Sa	12Ge	26Sa	1Ge	15Sa	19Ge	4Sa
July	3Ca	18Cp	22Ca	7Cp	11Ca	26Aq	30Ca	30Aq	19Ca	3Cp
August	1Le	16Aq	20 Le	6Ag	10Le	24Aq	29Vi	28Aq	17Le	2Cp
September	2Li	14Ar	18Vi	4Pi	8Vi	23Pi	27Vi	26Pi	16Vi	31Pi
October	28Li	14Ar	18Li	4Ar	7Li	23Ar	25Sc	26Ar	15Li	30Ar
November	27Sc	13Ta	16Sc	2Ar	6Sc	21Ta	25Sc	2Ta	13Sc	28Ta
December	27Cp	12Ge	16Sa	2Ta 31Ge	5Sa	21Ge	24Sa	10Ge	13Sa	28Ca

Key

Ar – Aries
Ta – Taurus
Ge – Gemini
Cn- Cancer
Le – Leo
Vi – Virgo
Li – Libra

Sc – Scorpio
Sg – Sagittarius
Cp – Capricorn
Aq - Aquarius
Pi - Pisces
NM-New Moon
FM-Full Moon

Resource Section

Practitioners
East Coast

Marcia Goodman-Blair, M.A.
Soul Spirit Journey
Reiki Master Teacher
Certified Crystal/Energy Healer
Astrological Counselor
New Hampshire
(603) 382-4725
http://www.soulpatterns.com

Dawna Memont
Serenity Center
Spiritual Counselor, Reiki Master,
Integration of Life Experience
Massachusetts,
(781) 231-3832
email: Serenity8140@aol.com

Nancy Smith
Angelscapes (intuitive drawings),
Reiki Master, Graphic Designer
Massachusetts
(978) 835-0005
http://www.angelscapes.com

Midwest

Ellen Costantino
CranioSacral Practitioner
Caledonia. Michigan
(616) 891-7578
email: ebcostantino@earthlink.net

Lisa Fryer
Astrologer, Tarot reader,
Ayurvedic Practitioner, Reiki
Dearborn, Michigan,
(313) 582-0999
email: moonchild93@prodigy.com

Laura Lohman-Gannan, DHM-CCH
Dr. of Homeopathy
Michigan
(248) 203-7123
email: officecall@aol.com

Crystal Jones
Massage Therapist, Aromatherapist
Mt Clemens, Michigan
(586) 465-6111

Laurie Pappas, Ph.D.
Metro Detroit Center for Attitudinal
Healing, Michigan
(248) 626-2312
email: lpapp3369@aol.com

Patty Shaw
Spiritual Counselor, Reiki Master
Redford, Michigan,
(313) 538-4142
email: pattypositively@netscape.net

Marc S. Terebelo, D.C.
Chiropractic Wellness Center
Michigan
(248) 569-0366

Stacey Theodossin
Ayurvedic Practitioner
Michigan
(866) 213-Heal, (248) 495-4325
email: healinggoddess@aol.com

Eve Wilson
Spiritual Counselor, Reiki Master,
Director of the nationally accredited
Healer Development Program
Royal Oak, Michigan
(248) 647-3241
http://www.spiritualhealers.com

Stacey Winn, D.C.
Main Street Chiropractic
Michigan
(586) 465-6111

West Coast

Sue Cielens
Certified Massage Therapist &
Licensed Physical Therapist,
Cranial Sacral Therapist
Colorado
(303) 941-4636

Neda Dardashti, R.P.P.
California
(310) 801-3455
neda@energyworkheals.com

Pat Donovan
Spiritual Counselor, Aromatherapist,
Certified Hypnotherapist,
Herbologist, Reiki Practitioner,
(928) 468-1078
www.talismanconsultingintl.com

Maureen McDonald
Tranquility Massage and Yoga Centers
California
For an appointment, (562) 760-1385
http://www.tranquilitymassage.com/
tranquility.htm

Schools

**Best websites for finding alternative
healing schools in your area, such as
Reiki, Massage, Acupuncture, Oriental
Medicine, Chiropractic, Ayurvedic,
Naturopathy and more.
http://www.naturalhealers.com
http://www.massagetherapy.net/
http://www.body-mind-spirit.com/

These listings are of professionals
dedicated to the health care industry
and in the field of therapeutic
massage. They are licensed per state
requirements and provide only health
care in the form of massage,
bodywork, and muscle therapy.

Massage Schools

East Coast

Delaware Learning Institute
Country Garden Business Center
Route 113, Box 144 D
Dagsboro, DE 19939
(888) 663-1121

Delaware Learning Institute
3515 Silver Side Road
Clayton Building, Suite 204
Wilmington, DE 19803
(888) 663-1121

**Philadelphia School of Massage
Therapy**
Washington Square West
6712 Washington Avenue,
Suite 309 (at Cardiff Circle)
Egg Harbor, NJ 08234
(856) 227-8363

**Philadelphia School of Massage
Therapy**
108-L Greentree Road and Black
Horse Pike
Turnersville, NJ 08012
(856) 227-8363

Virginia Learning Institute
7115 Leesburg Pike, Suite 315
Fallschurch, VA 22043
(703) 538-0800

South

Florida Key's Learning Institute
Hyatt Resort & Marina
601 Front Street
Key West, FL 33040
(800) 264-9835

Mid West

**Ann Arbor Institute of
Massage Therapy**
2835 Carpenter Rd.
Ann Arbor, MI 48108
(734) 677-4430
http://www.aaimt.com

Flint School of Therapeutic Massage
8240 Emburt, Grand Blanc, MI 48439
(810) 953-4811
http://www.fstm.com
email: fstm4u@aol.com

Health Enrichment Center, Inc.
School of Therapeutic Massage
204 E. Nepessing St.
Lapeer, MI 48446
(810) 667-9453
http://www.healthenrichment.com
email: hec@tir.com

Institute of Cognitive Behavorial Science
P.O. Box 74373
Romulus, MI 48174
(800) 850-5083

Irene's Myomassology Institute
26061 Franklin Rd.
Southfield, MI
(248) 350-1400
http://www.myomassology.com

Lakewood School of Therapeutic Massage
1102 6th Street
Port Huron, MI 48060
(810) 987-3959

Massage Therapy Program
10050 Roosevelt Boulevard
Philadelphia, PA 19116
(215) 969-1170
(800) 264-9835

Michigan School of Myomassology
3116 W. 12 Mile Rd.
Berkley, MI 48072
(248) 542-7228
fax: (248) 542-5830
http://www.therapeutic-touch.com

Pennsylvania Learning Institute
210 Montage Mountain Road
Moosic, PA 18507
(800) 264-9835

The Power of Touch
Somerset School of Massage Therapy
4290 Miller Road
Flint, MI
(810) 230-0353

Stressage Massage Institute
16587 Wyoming
Detroit, MI 48221
(313) 864-8355

West Coast

Alaska Learning Institute
Day's Inn
321 East 5th Avenue
Anchorage, AK 99501
(800) 264-9835

Brian Uttling School of Massage
900 Thomas St., Suite 200
Seattle, WA 98109
(800) 842-8731 or (206) 292-8055
http://www.busm.com
email: admissions@busm.com

IPSB · Cranial · Polarity Associate · Reflexology · Sports Massage
5817 Uplander Way
Culver City, CA 90230
(310) 342-9130
http://www.ipsb.com

Massage School and Healing Center
New Life Institute
The Town & Country Plaza
1159 Hilltop Dr., Redding, CA 96002
(530) 222-1467
http://www.newlifeinstitute.com

Milne Institute Inc.
P O Box 2716
Monterey, CA 93942-2716
(831) 649-1825

Oregon School of Massage
9500 SW Barbur Blvd., Suite 100
Portland, OR 97219
(503) 222-1467 or (800) 844-3420
http://www.oregonschoolof
massage.com

Reiki Certification Programs

East Coast

Soul Spirit Journey
Marcia Goodman-Blair, M.A.
Reiki Master Teacher,
Certified Crystal/Energy Healer,
Astrological Counselor
New Hampshire
(603) 382-4725
http://www.soulpatterns.com

Mid West

Center for Spiritual Development
21421 Hilltop #28
Southfield, MI 48034
(800) 322-8112 or (248) 948-8112
http://www.reiki.org
email: center@reiki.org

Eve Wilson
Royal Oak, MI
(248) 647-3241
http://www.spiritualhealers.com

Inner Light Services
Linda A Fischer
Sterling Heights, MI
(586) 215-7657
http://www.home.flash.net/~ilightsv

Reiki Healing Community
Southfield, MI
(248) 356-6110
email: Reikimim@aol.com

Cranial Sacral

Many Massage Therapists and
Chiropractic Doctors offer Cranial
Sacral Therapy

Ellen Costantino,
CranioSacral Practitioner
Caledonia. MI
(616) 891-7578
email: ebcostantino@earthlink.net

Chiropractic

Directory to help you find a
chiropractor in your city and state.
http://www.gnuhoo.com/Health/
Alternative/
http://www.naturalhealers.com/qa/
chiropractic.html

Beard Chiropractic Clinic
3815 Reveille
Houston, Texas 77087
Phone: (713) 649-2201
Fax: (713) 643-5521
http://web.wt.net/~autoclub

Chiropractic Wellness Center
Marc S. Terebelo, D.C.
26245 Southfield Rd
Lathrup Village. MI 48076
(248) 569-0366

Cleveland Chiropractic College
An independent not-for-profit
multicampus system of higher
education focused on preparing
Doctors of Chiropractic.
http://www.clevelandchiropractic.edu/

Main Street Chiropractic
Stacey Winn, D.C.
Mt. Clemens, Michigan
(586) 465-6111

Western States Chiropractic College
Portland, Oregon
http://www.wschiro.edu/

Aromatherapy

AromaWeb
Aromatherapy and essential oils site
for articles, recipes, synergies, listings.
http://www.aromaweb.com/

Ancient Healing Art -
PO Box 490
Placerville, CO 81430
(800) 537-1300 or (970) 728-1576
email: michele@AromaMarket.com

Aromaland Inc
1326 Rufina Circle
Santa Fe, NM 87505, USA
(800) 933-5267 0r (505) 438-0402
http://www.buyaromatherapy.com
email: sales@buyaromatherapy.com

Canadian National School of Aromatherapy
2505 Trondheim Crescent,
Mississauga,Ontario L5N 1P3
(905) 567-0422
email: cnsa@ica.net

Frontier Aromatherapy
Explore the aromatherapy glossary
and learn how the sense of smell
functions. Offers a newsletter and a
guide to essential oils.
http://www.frontierherb.com/

The National Association for Holistic Aromatherapy (NAHA)

NAHA News: The National
Association for Holistic
Aromatherapy (NAHA) is an
educational, nonprofit organization
dedicated to enhancing public
awarenesst of the benefits of true
aromatherapy.
http://www.naha.org/

Naturopathy

ALTERNATIVE Health News Online
Helpful alternative, complimentary,
and preventive health news that will
keep you up to date on the latest in
these rapidly growing fields.
http://www.altmedicine.com/

Clayton College of Natural Health
http://www.ccnh.edu/

Naturopathy Books
Reviews on Naturopathy Books
written by consumers at
http://www.epinions.com

Naturopathy Schools - A resource
and guide to schools of Naturopathy.
http://www.naturalHealers.com

National College of Naturopathic Medicine (NCNM)
Founded in 1956, the oldest
accredited school of natural medicine
in North America. The College has
been at the center of the profession,
preserving and extending the legacy
of naturopathic medicine.
http://www.ncnm.edu

Society of Naturopaths
Naturopathy Web Site
http://www.naturopath.org.nz/

Homeopathy

Laura Lohman-Gannan, DHM-CCH
Dr. of Homeopathy
Michigan
(248) 203-7123
email: officecall@aol.com

List of Homeopathic Schools and organizations
http://www.healthy.net/nch/index.html

The Medicine Garden, online
http://www.medicinegarden.com

National Center for Homeopathy
801 N. Fairfax Street, Suite 306
Alexandria, Virginia 22314
(877) 624-0613 or (703) 548-7790

North American Society of Homeopaths (NASH)
Directory of Registered Homeopaths
both in Canada and the USA.
http://www.homeopathy.org/

Yoga

http://www.yogadirectory.com
Links to websites of teachers, centers
and retreats.

http://www.yogajournal.com
A detailed directory and source guide.

http://www.yogafinder.com
This search engine will help you find websites categorized by state or instructor.

http://www.yogasite.com
A state by state listing of yoga instructors.

Healing Centers

MidWest

Bio Energy Medical Center
Michigan
(734) 995-3200

Creative Health Institute
The Wheatgrass Place – Health through Nutrition
918 Union City Road
Union City, MI 49094
(517) 278-6260

Healing Center
Featuring the Feldenkrais Method
586 S. Rochester
Rochester Hills, MI 48307
(248) 651-4537

Sinnett Holistic Health Services
Healing Touch Certification Program
221 E. Bloomfield
Royal Oak, MI 48037
Clinic: (248) 788-5808
School: (248) 302-3737
email: kathysinnett@compuserve.com

West Coast

Relaxation Now
Louise Goldberg, M.A.
PO Box 93-6123
Margate, FL 33093
email: lgfoss@aol.com
(954) 977-5035

Southern California Counseling Center
5615 West Pico Boulevard
Los Angeles, CA 90019
(323) 937-1344

The Total Health Connection, Inc.
123 N. San Vicente Blvd. Suite 123
Beverly Hills, CA 90211-2303
(323) 651-4531

Books

Astrology

The Complete Idiot's Guide to Astrology
by Madeline Gerwick-Brodeur and Lisa Lenard
Alpha Books

The Enchanted Astrologer
by Monte Farber
St. Martin Press

Your Magical Child
by Maria Kay Simms
ACS Publications

Channeling

Opening to Channel, How to Connect with Your Guide
by Sanaya Roman and Duane Packer
HJ Kramer Inc.

Energetic Medicine

Archangels and Earthangels
by, Petra Scheidner and Gerhard K. Peroth
Arcana Publishing

Bach Flower Remedies to the Rescue
by Gregory Valamis
Healing Arts Press

The Chakra System
by Anodea Judith (Audio)
Red Wheel/Weiser Publishing Co.

Chakra Therapy for Personal Growth and Healing
by Keith Sherwood
Llewellyn Publications

Color and Crystals, a Journey through the Chakras
by Joy Gardner
Crossing Press

The Crystal Handbook
by Kevin Sullivan
Publisher: Nal
Penguin Inc.

Crystal Healing, the Next Step
by Phyllis Galde
Llewellyn Publications

*Cunningham's Encyclopedia
of Crystal, Gem & Metal Magic*
by Scott Cunningham
Llewellyn Publications

*Essential Reiki, a Complete Guide
to an Ancient Healing Art*
by Diane Stein
Crossing Press

*Flower Essences and Vibrational
Healing*
by Gurudas
Cassandra Press

Gemisphere Luminary
by Michael Katz
Portland, Oregon

*Hands of Light, a Guide to Healing
Through the Human Energy Field*
by Barbara Ann Brennan
Bantam Books

Heal Your Body
by Louise L. Hay
Hay House

Healing on the Edge of Now
by Carl Brahe
Sunshine Press

Lightbeings – Master Essences
by Petra Scheidner
and Gerhard K. Peroth
Arcana Publishing

*Love is in the Earth, Reference Book
Describing the Metaphysical Properties
of the Mineral Kingdom*
by Melody
Earth Love Publication House

The Original Writings of Edward Bach
by Judy Howard and John Russel
C.W. Daniel Company Limited

*Personal Alchemy, a Handbook of
Healing and Self Transformation*
by Amber Wolf
Llewellyn Publications

The Personal Aura
by Dora van Gelder Kunz
Quest Books

Vibrational Medicine
by Richard Gerber, M.D.
Bear & Co.

Wheels of Life
by Anodea Judith
Llewellyn Publications

You Can Heal Your Life
by Louise L. Hay
Hay House

Health

The Body Knows
By Caroline M Sutherland
Hay House

*Herbs and Other Remedies,
the Ultimate Healing System*
by Donald Lepore, N.D.
Woodland Books

The Natural Remedy Book for Women
by Diane Stein
The Crossing Press

Prescription for Nutritional Healing
By James F. Balch, M.D. and Phyllus
A. Balch, C.N.C.
Avery Publishing Group

The Silent Passage
by Gail Sheehy
Simon & Schuster

Women's Body Women's Wisdom
by Christiane Northrup, M.D.
Bantam Books

The Yeast Connection
by Willam G. Crook, M.D.
Professional Book

You on a Diet
The Owners Manual for Waist
Management
by Michael F Roizen, M.D.
and Mehmet C. Oz, M.D.
Free Press

Homeopathy

The Complete Family Guide to
Homeopathy
by Dr. Christopher Hammond,
MB, BS, LCH
Penquin Books USA, Inc.

Emotional Healing with Homeopathy,
A Self Help Manual
by Peter Chappell,
BSc, RSHom, Fshom,
Element Books Limited

Human Condition: Critical
by Luc De Schepper, M.D., Ph.D.,
Lic. Ac., D.I. Hom., C. Hom.
Full of Life Publishing

The People's Repertory
by Luc De Schepper, M.D., Ph.D.,
Lic. Ac., D.I. Hom., C. Hom.
Full of Life Publishing

Hypnotherapy

Many Lives Many Masters
by Brian Weiss, M.D.
Publisher: Simon & Schuster

Scars of the Soul, Holistic Healing in
the Edgar Cayce Readings
by Mary Anne Woodward
Brindabella Books

Life after Death

Echoes of the Soul
by Echo Bodine
New World Library

Embraced by the Light
by Betty J. Eadie
Bantam Books

Relax, It's only a Ghost
by Echo Bodine
Element Books

A Soul's Journey, Whispers
from the Light
by Patricia Idol
New Falcon Publications

Nutrition/Cookbooks

Diet for a Small Planet
by Frances Moore Lappe'
Ballantine Books

Eat Right for Your Type
by Peter J.D'Adamo
and Cathrine Whitney
G.P. Putnam's Sons

Fit for Life
by Harvey and Marilyn Diamond
Warner Books

Recipes for a Small Planet
by Ellen Buchman Ewald
Ballantine Books

Rodale's Basic Natural Foods Cookbook
by Charles Gerras, Editor
A Fireside Book published by Simon
& Schuster

Psychic Protection

Psychic Protection
by Ted Andrews
Dragonhawk Publishing

Psychic Self Defense
By Dion Fortune
Weiser Books

Psychic Shield: The Personal Handbook
of Psychic Protection
by Caitlin Matthews
Ulysses Press

Reliance on the Light
by Diane Stein
Crossing Press

Ritual/Divination

Angel Blessings – Cards of Sacred
Guidance and Inspiration
by Kimberly Marooney
Merrill West Publishing Company

The Angel Tarot
by Rosemary Ellen Guilet
and Robert Michael Place
Harper, San Fransisco

The Crystal Ally Cards
by Naisha Ashsia
Heaven and Earth Publishing Co.

The Healing Runes
by Ralph H.Blum
and Susan Loughan
St. Martins Press

Inner Child Cards
by Isha Lerner
and Mark Lernaer
Bear & Company, Sante Fe, NM

Medicine Cards
by Jamie Sams
and David Carson
Bear & Company. Sante Fe, NM

Oracle of the Goddess
by Amy Zerner and Monte Farber
St Martin Press

Shamanism

The Way of the Shaman
by Michael Harner
Harper Collins

*In the Shadow of the Shaman
Connecting with Self, Nature & Spirit*
by Amber Wolfe
Llewellyn

*Mending the Past and Healing the
Future with Soul Retrieval*
by Alberto Volloldo, Ph.D.
Hay House

Spiritual Inspiration

The Art of Happiness
by The Dali Lama
and Howard C. Cutler, M.D.
Riverhead Books, a member of
Penguin Putnam Inc.

Care of the Soul
by Thomas Moore
Harper Perennial

The Celestine Prophecy
by James Redfield
Warner Books

*The Celestine Vision, Living the New
Spiritual Awareness*
by James Redfield
Warner Books Inc.

*Conversations with God:
Books One, Two and Three*
by Neal Donald Walsch
G.P. Putnam's Son's

The Emissary of Light
by James F. Twyman
Findhorn Press

The Greatest Salesman in the World
by Og Mandino
Bantam Books

Iron John, a Book about Men
by Robert Bly,
Vintage Books

The Messengers
by Julia Ingram and G.W Hardin
Pocket Books

The Next Step
by Patricia Diane Cota-Robles
The New Age Study of Humanities
Purpose, Inc.

*Reflections of the Christ Mind,
the Present-Day Teaching of Jesus*
by Paul Ferrini
Doubleday

A Return to Love
by Marianne Williamson
Harper Perennial

The Road Less Traveled
by Scott Peck, M.D.
Simon and Schuster

Seat of the Soul
by Gary Zukav
Fireside Book
Simon and Schuster

The Secret of the Beloved Disciple
by James F. Twyman
Findhorn Press

The Sermon on the Mount, the Key to Success in Life
by Emmet Fox

The Tenth Insight
by James Redfield
Time Warner Books

Visionary Business
by Marc Allen
New World Library

A Woman's Worth
by Marianne Williamson
Harper Perennial

Spirituality for Children and Young Adults

Meditating with Children
by Deborah Rozman
University of the Trees Press

Mountain, Meadows and Moonbeams
by Mary Summer Rain
Hampton Roads Publishing Co, Inc.

The Young Old Masters, a Spiritual Guide for Young and Old
by Chris Wagner, Ph.D.
and Mary Norris, M.S.W.
Ohm Press

Notes:

Notes:

Winding Road
PUBLISHING INC.

Quick Order Form

Fax Orders: (248) 546-8480 – Send this form.

Telephone Orders: Call (800) 810-3837 or (248) 545-8360
Please have your credit card ready.

Email Orders: healersalmanac@aim.com
www.coventrycreations.com

Postal Orders: Winding Road Publishing, Inc.
2355 Wolcott, Ferndale, MI 48220 USA,
Attention: Patty Shaw

Please send _____ copies of Healer's Almanac, Goddess Edition, $18.95 each, plus shipping and handling.

Sales tax: Please add 6% for books shipped to Michigan addresses

Payment & Billing Address:

Visa _____ Mastercard _____ Expiration Date: _____

Card number: _____

Name on Card: _____

Address of Cardholder: _____

City: _____ State: _____ Zip: _____

Telephone: _____

Email: _____

Shipping Address (if different):

Name: _____

Address: _____

City: _____ State: _____ Zip: _____

Telephone: _____